Intelligent Document Capture with Ephesoft

Learn to use open source software to automate the processing of scanned and digital documents to save time, save money, and improve accuracy

Pat Myers

Ike Kavas

Michael Muller

Clifford Laurin

[PACKT] PUBLISHING

open source
community experience distilled

BIRMINGHAM - MUMBAI

Intelligent Document Capture with Ephesoft

First published: September 2012

Production Reference: 1060912

Published by Packt Publishing Ltd.
Livery Place
35 Livery Street
Birmingham B3 2PB, UK.

ISBN 978-1-84969-372-1

www.packtpub.com

Cover Image by iStockPhoto

Credits

Foreword

In my recent e-book #*OccupyIT: A Technology Manifesto for the Cloud, Mobile, and Social Era* (http://www.aiim.org/occupyIT), I talk about the revolutionary changes that are impacting how we make enterprise technology decisions.

On the one hand, we have "the business," awed and impressed by the changes and speed of implementation in the consumer technology space (think Facebook, Google, Twitter), asking their IT departments why enterprise technology has to be so "old fashioned," why implementation needs to take so long, and why enterprise technology has to be so darn expensive.

On the other hand, we have "IT", struggling to maintain order amidst the chaos, and struggling with expectations from "the business" that are escalating exponentially. IT spending by IT is flat, while IT spending by "the business" is increasing significantly. Clearly the traditional world of enterprise IT is changing.

In many ways, the cloud and open source revolutions are two sides of the same coin. They stem from the desire to buy technology "by the glass," to buy technology in which the release cycles are frequent and manageable rather than long and frightening, and you can "try before you buy" (and especially before you scale!).

According to a recent global CIO survey, 60 percent of organizations are ready to embrace cloud computing over the next five years as a means of growing their businesses and achieving a competitive advantage. The figure is nearly twice the number of CIOs who said they would utilize the cloud in the previous study.

The impact of the cloud and open source, though, will be massive beyond the immediate revenues that will be classified in industry studies as cloud and open source because they fundamentally change the way we look at IT services, how we pay for these services within our organization (capital spending versus operating), and how we view upgrade paths (and who is responsible for these upgrades). Organizations that do not incorporate rapid and flexible implementation and adoption models into their thinking do so at their own peril.

This frame of flexibility and rapid deployment is how we need to think about an aspect of the content management industry that has been with us for a long time; capture.

No matter how elegant the frontend, Systems of Engagement (for a white paper on this, see http://aiim.org/futurehistory) cannot operate in an environment in which the processes that support and complement these Systems of Engagement are engulfed by paper and inefficiency. The reality is that most organizations exist in a hybrid environment in which process information may come from paper documents, paper forms, web forms, faxes, telephony, e-mails, SMS, mobile, and social.

Automated capture of information as early as possible in the business process and as close to the point of origination produces cleaner data, resulting in higher quality information, less exception handling, and better process management. The more important the process is to a business, the greater the impact such improvements will have. Once paper-based information moves into the digital realm it can be used to enrich social and mobile applications. In paper form, that information might as well not exist since no one can get to it without great effort.

The reality that exists in most organizations suggests that although capture and its associated technologies are mature technologies, the market and the scale of implementation is anything but.

According to a recent AIIM study (Automating Financial Processes: User Feedback on the Real ROI), the average cost to process a paper invoice is still more than $9. Overall, 52 percent of organizations surveyed have yet to adopt any automated AP systems. One third of organizations receiving more than 25,000 invoices per month are still using paper-based processes.

These findings were reaffirmed in a follow-up AIIM survey (Process Revolution: Moving Your Business from Paper to PC to Tablet). A third of small and mid-sized companies and 22 percent of the largest have yet to adopt any paper-free processes. Only 20 percent of organizations of any size proactively evaluate all processes for driving out paper. The percentage of processes that could be paper free is actually only 14 percent. Seventy-seven percent of invoices that arrive as PDF attachments get printed. Thirty-one percent of faxed invoices get printed and scanned back in.

I could go on and on. Perhaps the most astonishing thing about all of this is how compelling the ROI actually is for scanning and capture – once people can be convinced to make the jump.

Per Process Revolution, on average respondents using scanning and capture consider that it improves the speed of response to customers, suppliers, citizens, or staff by six times or more. Seventy percent estimate an improvement of at least three times, and nearly a third (29 percent) sees an improvement of 10 times or more. Forty-two percent of users have achieved a payback period of 12 months or less from their scanning and capture investments. Fifty-seven percent are posting a payback of 18 months or less.

So the opportunity is there. I am convinced we can all do a better job of educating decision-makers about new cloud and open source models for delivering capture and content management technologies. I am also convinced that we can all do a better job of educating decision-makers about the benefits of capture and how to implement capture systems quickly and effectively. Hence, my great pleasure in writing the foreword to this book.

John Mancini,
Author, Speaker, and President of AIIM

About the Authors

Pat Myers is the Executive Vice President and a co-founder of Zia Consulting, a content centric solutions firm. Zia is a platinum Ephesoft and Alfresco partner that provides solutions from paper to mobile. Pat has over 10 years of Enterprise Content Management experience and 15 years of professional services and application development experience. Pat and Ike developed the official Ephesoft training.

> I would like to thank my wife Margaret for giving me unconditional love and encouragement in everything I do, my daughter Zoe for making me remember what is important in life, and my God for giving me so many opportunities. Additionally, I would like to thank my extended family and friends for making my life so enjoyable. I would also like to thank my Zia family for making me want to go to work every day and achieve greatness.

Ike Kavas has more than 12 years of solid experience in document imaging, document management, workflow, and systems. Mr. Kavas is the founder and the Chief Technology Officer at Ephesoft, Inc., responsible for product design and roadmap. He is a serial entrepreneur with three successful companies. He has both a keen technical background, which he developed by implementing several multimillion dollar projects for a fortune 100 companies, and has outstanding sales and business experience, which he demonstrated by achieving and exceeding revenue-based goals.

Before founding Ephesoft, Inc., Mr. Kavas managed professional services at Kofax, Inc. and co-founded other technology companies in southern California. Mr. Kavas holds a Bachelor of Science degree in Electronics & Electrical Engineering and CDIA+ certification.

I would like to thank my family for all the support they have given me, namely, Birsen Kavas, Fuat Kavas, and my wife Melanie Kavas.

I would like to thank my Ephesoft team for creating and maintaining such a great product and helping us bring this technology to the marketplace.

Michael Muller is Director of Engineering at Zia Consulting. He has 25 years of professional software development experience, currently specializing in enterprise content management.

Clifford Laurin has over 17 years of professional experience as a software engineer, including 11 years in the field of Enterprise Content Management. He is currently an ECM Architect at Zia Consulting.

About the Reviewers

Eric Harper is the Director of Software Consulting at Zia Consulting. He has several years of software development and consulting experience in content management, customer relationship management, web application development, and data warehousing. Prior to Zia, Eric was a co-founder and chief architect of the CRM services startup eConvergent where he led the software development team through an acquisition by the analytics and credit scoring leader, FICO.

Megan Hoffman is a Project Manager at Zia Consulting and has over 10 years of experience implementing and managing software solutions. Throughout her career she has held a variety of positions including business analyst, project manager, and product manager. Having had some experience writing software training material in the past, Megan was excited to take on the project manager and reviewer roles for this initiative.

Anita L. Feeley is a Project Manager living in Nederland, Colorado. Anita has over 14 years of experience with software implementations including project management, business analysis, testing, reporting, and training as well as database management and XSL stylesheet creation. She has worked in the insurance and financial industries as well as with government agencies. Anita has an M.A. from the University of Maryland and enjoys reading, biking, hiking, and spending time with her family in the mountains.

Alicia Libucha has 15 years of technical marketing and communications experience specializing in media/analyst relations, customer programs, and social media. During that time, she has worked with leading enterprise software companies in the document management, imaging, mobile, and security space.

www.PacktPub.com

Support files, eBooks, discount offers and more

You might want to visit www.PacktPub.com for support files and downloads related to your book.

Did you know that Packt offers eBook versions of every book published, with PDF and ePub files available? You can upgrade to the eBook version at www.PacktPub.com and as a print book customer, you are entitled to a discount on the eBook copy. Get in touch with us at service@packtpub.com for more details.

At www.PacktPub.com, you can also read a collection of free technical articles, sign up for a range of free newsletters and receive exclusive discounts and offers on Packt books and eBooks.

http://PacktLib.PacktPub.com

Do you need instant solutions to your IT questions? PacktLib is Packt's online digital book library. Here, you can access, read and search across Packt's entire library of books.

Why Subscribe?

- Fully searchable across every book published by Packt
- Copy and paste, print and bookmark content
- On demand and accessible via web browser

Free Access for Packt account holders

If you have an account with Packt at www.PacktPub.com, you can use this to access PacktLib today and view nine entirely free books. Simply use your login credentials for immediate access.

Table of Contents

Preface

Enterprise content management tools help large organizations process large quantities of documents. There are many components involved in a comprehensive content management solution; a repository stores the organization's documents, a workflow engine facilitates business processes, and a records management tool ensures compliance with your organization's document retention requirements. These tools all assume an understanding of the documents that they're managing; they must be able to distinguish an invoice from a loan application, and know that invoices have purchase order numbers on them, and that loan applications have social security numbers.

Therefore, prior to sending your documents to your organization's enterprise tools, you must identify the document type and enter any associated "metadata" (like the purchase order number). Without Ephesoft, this is an expensive, manual, time-consuming, and error-prone process.

Ephesoft automates document type identification and the extraction of metadata. In this book, we teach you to use Ephesoft to save time, save money, and improve the quality of the information in your organization's enterprise tools.

What this book covers

Chapter 1: Introduction, introduces Ephesoft and intelligent document capture.

Chapter 2: A Quick Tour of Ephesoft, covers a walk-through of Ephesoft's user interface.

Chapter 3: Creating a Batch Class, covers learning to set up Ephesoft.

Chapter 4: Processing a Batch, covers learning to use Ephesoft.

Chapter 5: Core Ephesoft Features, covers expanding on the features introduced in *Chapter 3*.

Chapter 6: Ephesoft Extended Features, covers learning advanced Ephesoft features.

Chapter 7: Tips, includes productivity enhancing tips.

Appendix: Reference, includes some reference material.

What you need for this book

You will need Ephesoft Enterprise 3.0+ running on a Windows box.

Who this book is for

This book is intended for information technology professionals interested in installing and configuring Ephesoft for their organization, but it is a valuable resource for anyone interested in learning about document capture in general.

Conventions

In this book, you will find a number of styles of text that distinguish between different kinds of information. Here are some examples of these styles, and an explanation of their meaning.

Code words in text are shown as follows: "You can use generic variables, which are EphesoftBatchID and EphesoftDOCID."

A block of code is set as follows:

```
import com.ephesoft.dcma.da.id.BatchInstanceID;
public interface SamplePluginService {
  void sampleMethod(BatchInstanceID batchInstanceID,
      final String pluginWorkflow) throws Exception;
}
```

New terms and **important words** are shown in bold. Words that you see on the screen, in menus or dialog boxes for example, appear in the text like this: "Administrators can use the **Up** and **Down** buttons to reorder the plugins or the **Remove** button to remove plugins from the module."

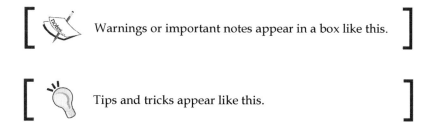

Warnings or important notes appear in a box like this.

Tips and tricks appear like this.

Reader feedback

Feedback from our readers is always welcome. Let us know what you think about this book—what you liked or may have disliked. Reader feedback is important for us to develop titles that you really get the most out of.

To send us general feedback, simply send an e-mail to feedback@packtpub.com, and mention the book title through the subject of your message.

If there is a topic that you have expertise in and you are interested in either writing or contributing to a book, see our author guide on www.packtpub.com/authors.

Customer support

Now that you are the proud owner of a Packt book, we have a number of things to help you to get the most from your purchase.

Errata

Although we have taken every care to ensure the accuracy of our content, mistakes do happen. If you find a mistake in one of our books—maybe a mistake in the text or the code—we would be grateful if you would report this to us. By doing so, you can save other readers from frustration and help us improve subsequent versions of this book. If you find any errata, please report them by visiting http://www.packtpub.com/support, selecting your book, clicking on the **errata submission form** link, and entering the details of your errata. Once your errata are verified, your submission will be accepted and the errata will be uploaded to our website, or added to any list of existing errata, under the Errata section of that title.

Piracy

Piracy of copyright material on the Internet is an ongoing problem across all media. At Packt, we take the protection of our copyright and licenses very seriously. If you come across any illegal copies of our works, in any form, on the Internet, please provide us with the location address or website name immediately so that we can pursue a remedy.

Please contact us at copyright@packtpub.com with a link to the suspected pirated material.

We appreciate your help in protecting our authors, and our ability to bring you valuable content.

Questions

You can contact us at questions@packtpub.com if you are having a problem with any aspect of the book, and we will do our best to address it.

1
Introduction

Ephesoft is an open source intelligent document capture product offered by Ephesoft, Inc. Ephesoft classifies and separates page images into documents and extracts metadata from the **Optical Character Recognition (OCR)** content of a document. The web-based user interface allows operators to review documents and validate extracted content. The assembled documents and their associated metadata can be exported to other **enterprise content management (ECM)** systems for further processing.

If that explanation didn't make any sense, fear not; in this first chapter we will introduce you to the basics of intelligent document capture also known as **document capture** by walking you through the following topics:

- Overview of document capture
- History of document capture
- Elements of document capture projects
- Inside a capture system
- What sets document capture apart from other ECM tools

Overview

Organizations need tools to manage their information, or knowledge. Document management, workflow, web content management, document capture, records management, portals, and other knowledge management systems are a few of the tools categorized as enterprise content management, or ECM. Since information or knowledge can be stored in many different electronic systems, these ECM tools communicate not only with each other, but also with other corporate systems such as **enterprise resource planning (ERP)** systems, accounting systems, **customer relationship management (CRM)**, and other assorted databases.

ECM is a combination of tools to manage information or knowledge for organizations.

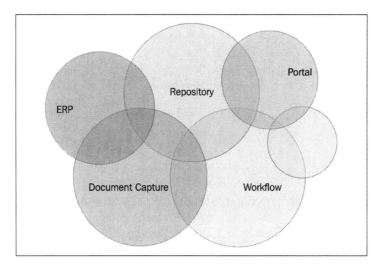

This book focuses specifically on one of these tools—document capture. More specifically, we will examine how Ephesoft is used to implement document capture systems.

Document capture deals with transforming paper documents to electronic files using devices such as scanners and cameras, and turning electronic files into meaningful data. The combined electronic file and its metadata can be stored in repositories such as document management systems or electronic records management systems. Some users employ a *Scan to Archive* approach but the same technology can also be used to drive other electronic systems that require further processing, often called *Scan to Process*.

As an example, ACME insurance company receives an application form to open a new account. The form is completed by the new customer and signed. A document capture system is used to scan the document into an electronic file, typically in a TIFF or PDF format. The document capture system is also used to extract valuable data that the new customer has entered on the paper application form. This could include name, address, and social security number. At this stage, the document capture system has the following two sets of information:

- An electronic file version of the paper document
- The metadata information that is extracted from the electronic file

ACME insurance company can use this information in two ways: it can store the file and its data in a repository for archival purposes; or it can send the data to the new accounts department for further processing.

Note that document capture may not always include scanning as some documents are already in electronic files. In these cases, document capture is only responsible for classification and extracting the data from the document.

For example, a computer accessories company sells its products to schools. Every time a school needs a product, they fax or email the orders to the company. The computer accessories company receives the orders via its fax servers or receives them into a designated e-mail inbox. Document capture systems can monitor the fax servers and e-mail inboxes to capture the metadata such as order number, school name, and even tables of line items with the specific part numbers and quantities that are ordered.

History of document capture

Document imaging started in the 1980s using specialized hardware for both transforming paper documents to images and recognizing the textual content (using OCR) on machine printed documents. Over time, its widespread use on Microsoft Windows systems helped to commoditize document capture software.

The ability to identify documents and capture OCR metadata from pre-defined locations on paper spurred an advanced form of capture called fixed form processing. Documents such as credit card application forms, insurance claim forms, or simple survey forms are now designed with soft colors or boxes to constrain letters for improved intelligent character recognition (ICR) of hand-written characters. These applications also use special markers to register the document. Registering documents allows software to save the position of the fields and also identify the document type so that the software can extract the field values from predefined locations (x-y coordinates).

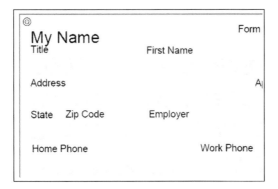

In the early days of document capture, systems relied on separator sheets or barcodes to classify and separate documents. Users had to insert special sheets with markings on them to designate where a document started and ended. The main reason for this was to improve efficiency because production scanners can scan hundreds of pages per minute. Adding separator sheets was faster than scanning documents one by one.

The next wave of software applications tried to eliminate the need to design special forms to capture fields and identify the document type. We call these intelligent document capture systems because the systems try to locate the data intelligently. For example, these systems find the invoice date by locating words like "Date" or "Invoice" on the document to locate the actual invoice date value.

Today, intelligent document capture systems are able to extract more challenging content, using new techniques including:

- Automatically extracting tables of line items from various documents without configuring each and every one of the document types or vendors sending the documents. These systems use either table headers or the format of the columns or both to determine the presence of a table and then extract the data.

- Matching documents to database records. For example, consider an insurance company that receives faxes from its customers. Intelligent document capture systems can analyze all the words on the faxes and use names, addresses, and phone numbers (even if they are partially available) to determine the customer ID because the insurance company already has a database with all this information.

- Content analysis to classify documents, as opposed to using markers or rules that make a decision based on a few words. This feature not only classifies documents but also automatically decides where each document starts and ends which can eliminate the labor-intensive step of using barcodes to classify and separate documents. Consider a hospital that scans patient records. Each patient may have dozens of documents, each of which is several pages long. Instead of placing barcode-based separator pages manually between every document before scanning them, new intelligent document capture products can analyze the content of each page to decide where each document starts and stops while also deciding what type of document it is processing, for example, lab report, admission form, or nurse's note.

Elements of document capture projects

There are three aspects to a document capture project. They are as follows:

- The destination of the documents
- The location of the documents and systems
- The type of documents to be processed

The destination of the documents

Document capture systems can be categorized in the following two ways:

- **Scan to archive**: These are documents that are scanned into repositories for long-term storage with easy access. The main purpose for this is to maintain archives. For example, a hospital may scan patient records into an electronic records management system to keep a permanent archive. Scan to archive projects generally are implemented in the following two ways:
  - **Backfile conversion**: Transforming old paper documents into meaningful electronic data.
  - **Day-Forward conversion**: Transforming current paper documents for immediate use.
- **Scan to business process (scan to workflow)**: Documents that are scanned to initiate a business process or other workflows are considered scan to business process. For example, scanning an invoice to an invoice approval system (a business process), or scanning a credit card application form in a bank branch to begin an account opening workflow would be considered a *scan to business process* project.

The value of understanding these project types occurs when you consider their importance to the organization. Scan to archive projects are generally implemented to access or preserve the documents and information. In many cases, converting the documents to online information empowers companies to find information and make better use of it. An equally important feature is preventing its loss in case of a disaster.

Scan to process projects generally focus on improving business processes. By definition, these types of projects are focused on saving money, improving productivity, or improving customer response time, thus making them more valuable to customers since the **return on investment** (**ROI**) can be calculated.

The location of the documents and systems

It is important to know where documents are and where they need to be located in order to be processed. Large organizations may find that forming a document processing service center is more economical than having document capture dispersed through their organization. For example, an insurance company may be able to advise all its customers and vendors to send their documents and correspondence to one mailing address, which allows them to have a central document processing center. On the other hand, a bank with 500 branch offices cannot tell customers who come to a branch office to open an account that they now need to send the documents to a central mailing address. The branch needs to provide full service to the customer and handle their immediate needs. In this case, branch personnel are responsible for capturing the documents. The bank then needs to decide if the documents will be processed locally or forwarded to a central document processing center.

Most organizations have opted for a centralized approach since having systems and employees at each branch to process documents may be too costly. But how do the documents arrive at the central site? The traditional approach has been to use internal company mail services or private carriers like FedEx or UPS. This can be quite expensive if done daily. An alternative is to scan or fax the documents with minimal information such as an account number. The documents would then be electronically forwarded to the central location. This approach is called **distributed document capture**.

There are a number of options organizations may choose from based on how they intend to implement document capture within their infrastructure. They are as follows:

- **Document processing service centers**: These centers are designed to host document capture software, hardware (such as high-speed scanners, fax machines, and so on), technical support personnel, and document processing operators. From an infrastructure perspective, having everything in a single location is desirable. Some organizations build replica systems in different geographic locations for disaster recovery and business continuity purposes. The advantage with this approach is that organizations can save money by maintaining one system and having employees dedicated to one process to improve efficiency and accuracy.

- **Distributed document capture**: An alternative to a centralized approach is to distribute the workload. Documents are scanned and processed where the documents originate. The advantage of these systems is a reduction of the mailing or transportation costs, and increasing the speed of transforming the documents into meaningful information.

- **Hybrid systems**: It is possible to combine the two methods previously listed to gain the advantages of both options. By creating a handful of service centers and allowing documents to be scanned at the origination, organizations not only maintain fewer systems but also distribute the work between data centers. Documents can be scanned where they originate and can be electronically forwarded to one of the centers for processing.

- **Cloud systems**: Could a company have only one document capture system where all the service centers and document origination sites, even consumers, could access and share the workload? The answer is yes, by using a cloud system. Whether it's an internal cloud or an external cloud doesn't matter. Cloud systems can take the hybrid approach to the next level and create a document capture platform for organizations to achieve the best of all the options above. Ephesoft provides a cloud-ready capture platform that can process all document types coming into any organization's mailrooms.

The type of documents to be processed

What do you receive in your mailroom? Organizations receive a variety of documents such as invoices, orders, assorted forms, correspondence, legal contracts, and human resource documents. Document capture systems should be able to process all the documents an organization receives regardless of the format or size. This is especially true for organizations that have service centers, which are designed to handle documents received from all the departments in a large company. In most cases document capture solutions are only installed to automate the documents for a specific department or business process.

By analyzing specific business processes, we can understand the different technologies needed to handle the documents. Some examples are as follows:

- **Mortgage loan processing**: There are 200 to 400 different types of mortgage documents. Some document types are one-page documents and some are 50 pages and more. Since documents come from a variety of sources, such as bank statements or lease/rental agreements, document capture systems should be able to handle the small variances. The traditional way to classify these documents was to have employees insert separator sheets with bar or patch codes between each of the different document types. As a result, a single loan package could end up with 200 or more different separator sheets. The separator sheet method is accurate if employees are skilled and diligent but it requires thorough training and expensive labor. An alternative is to set up rules to capture certain keywords and use them to separate documents. Rules-based systems are good for a relatively small number of document types. If you have more than 20 document types, not to mention 200, it becomes a maintenance nightmare for the organization to manage and ensure accuracy. The best way to separate and classify mortgage documents is to perform a content analysis of each page. Ephesoft utilizes the Lucene search engine to identify which document type is being processed. With this information, Ephesoft can not only tell where the documents start and end, but also what the document type is without separator sheets and without the need for rules. Ephesoft only needs a few samples of each document type to compare the content. This type of classification is best for organizations receiving a variety of documents from different sources such as a bank mailroom, an insurance mailroom, a hospital patient records department, human resources in a large firm, and so on.

- **Claims processing**: In the United States, every health insurance company uses government-issued forms to pay their bills. The fixed forms are designed as color dropout, perfect for Zonal OCR and ICR, as well as handwriting recognition. As discussed earlier, fixed form processing has been around for many years. Document capture systems can handle color dropout, and black and white forms, and allow administrators to specify field-level properties such as numeric-only fields, remove boxes, field-level ignore areas, and so on. Since these documents do not change, using barcode or content analysis as a classification technique is unnecessary. In this case, document capture is configured either to use one fixed document type by default or use image (also called Layout) classification.

- **Invoices** and **sales orders**: The challenge with invoices and purchase orders are twofold:

  ° Classification and separation: If a multi-page invoice is received, the only way to identify where the document starts and ends is to look at the page number or invoice total. This means that classification depends on extraction of the metadata.

  ° Extraction: Invoices and orders may come from thousands of different sources making it harder to extract or capture the data. This applies to regular fields such as `dates`, `order number`, and `total amount` due. It also applies to more difficult fields like `ship-to` address and table/line items.

For many of these business processes, the most common way to solve the classification and separation challenge is to use separator sheets or barcodes. For example, one can stamp a barcode or place a sticker with a barcode on every first page of the invoice. However, more elegant solutions can be utilized by extracting the data. For example, document capture systems can capture the invoice or order number from every page and determine where the documents start and end without any labor. Please note that this method may not be 100 percent accurate and a quality control system such as Ephesoft's Document Review Module should be used to ensure zero false positives.

Extraction of the fields requires different techniques to capture multiple field types. Capturing main fields such as invoice number, order number, total, VAT, invoice date, and ship date is easy. Many capture systems like Ephesoft allow you to set rules such as "Find the phrase "Invoice Date", look around it and capture the value that looks like a date". Furthermore, some systems can also learn to automatically create and store rules and important information about these fields.

Capturing table/line items relies on content analysis at a different level. Capture systems can recognize the table and column structures and map them to predefined columns from an external data source, such as an ERP system. Technologies in this area are still evolving. The challenge all document capture companies are trying to solve is not only to deal with different formats of the tables but also how to map them to external data sources. For example, line items containing part numbers and hourly services performed do not generally match identically to the corresponding data elements in the accounting or ERP system.

Capturing "vendor" or "ship to" information is another challenge. Document capture vendors traditionally find ways to locate this type of information by capturing phone or fax numbers, names, or even city, state and zip combinations but some, including Ephesoft, use additional techniques to find this data if the customer has a database that can be accessed. For example, the Ephesoft **FUZZY DB** matching plugin allows Ephesoft to analyze all the words to see if there is a match in the vendor table from the ERP system. This makes it very easy to find the addressees or vendor information accurately and fast.

Inside a capture system

Capture systems, including Ephesoft, automate classification and data entry of documents, and deliver this data to other systems. Capture systems are not content repositories; their job is to transform the document into information as soon as possible and give it to repositories or other processes.

To accomplish this, capture systems use an internal workflow system. In general, this is a linear workflow and includes the following steps: Import, Classify, Extract, and Export. Let us analyze these major steps:

Import methods

Capture solutions need the flexibility to ingest images from different sources. Common methods include the following:

- **Scanners**:

    Scanning options include:

    - **Low speed scanners**: These scanners are used on a personal or departmental level, and can scan up to 50 pages per minute. They are generally small enough to fit on office desks so that users can scan their own documents for the business process.

    - **High speed scanners**: These scanners are used to scan thousands of pages daily and are operated by dedicated scan operators at service centers or service bureaus. They can scan up to 200 pages per minute, duplex, and include special features to make the scanning process as efficient as possible. For example, many can detect double-page scanning and warn the user if a page is missed during scanning.

- ◦ **Very high speed scanners**: These scanners are used to scan thousands of pages every hour. One scanner could be 6-8 feet long and may require more than one operator. Very high speed scanners often come with special software to help aid the users. These scanners are designed to process millions of documents and are generally found in large mailrooms or service centers.

- ◦ **Multi-Function Printer (MFP)**: These are the machines that combine copy, print, fax, and scan into one device. They are generally not designed for high speed or high quality scanning but are very popular because of their ease of use and convenience. An advantage of these devices is that users can scan the document to a folder; they can e-mail it or even FTP it to a central location. Some MFPs allow you to configure the user screen to allow easy scanning to specific business processes.

- ◦ **Network attached scanners**: These scanners, similar to MFPs, do not require a computer to scan documents, thus providing a great convenience. They carry the same qualities of the MFPs but since they are focused only on scanning (no copying or printing), they typically have better scanning quality than MFPs. By providing customizations, they offer scan to process for remote scanning.

- ◦ **Specialty scanners**: This group includes scanners that can open envelopes and scanners that can scan books without taking the binders off.

- **Fax machines** or **Electronic fax servers**: Electronic fax servers are used by many organizations to transform paper documents to electronic files, to save money on scanning and transportation expenses. Although they can be very cost effective, organizations need to be careful about extraction accuracy and automation rates. Many document capture systems can get better recognition rates when using scanners. Even if the accuracy difference is less than 10 percent, it may mean millions of dollars and ten times extra employees for any organization processing millions of documents every year.

- **E-mail servers**: Document capture systems can not only import the e-mails and their attachments but also convert those documents to image formats such as TIFF or PDF to eliminate the need for printing and scanning them.

- **Print streams** or **EDI files**: Communication between companies sometimes relies on exchanging files such as **Electronic Data Interchange (EDI)** files. Although these files are great for processing and transferring data, a document capture system can be used to convert the EDI file to a visual representation so that when users need to access it or process it, they can see or retrieve the document just as any other document in the repository or business process.

- **Mobile devices**: Mobile device adoption is increasing especially for companies where field officers or employees or consumers rely on these devices to capture documents. For example, some companies allow you to take pictures of your checks and deposit them right from your mobile phone.

Classification methods

Capture solutions require different methods of classification that can be used depending on the format and commonality of the images being processed. These include the following:

- **Barcode/patch code**: Classifying and separating documents based on special barcodes. These barcodes can reside on a separate page called separator pages or they can be placed on the first page of every document. Ephesoft utilizes one or two-dimensional barcodes such as QR, 3 of 9, and Data Matrix to achieve this. QR codes are the recommended method for the following two reasons:

    ◦ Other barcodes such as 3 of 9 and Data Matrix are commonly used on documents for other purposes and can confuse the capture system

    ◦ QR codes are less prone to error

- **Image/Layout classification**: Some documents can be easily classified based on their layouts. For example, one can see the difference between a credit card application form and a correspondence letter from 10 meters. This method works well for documents with unchanged structure and with finite pages. For example, Ephesoft uses this technique in a claim processing solution to differentiate between black and white, and color dropout medical claims.

- **Extraction based classification**: Documents can also be classified based on keywords. For example, one can configure the document capture system to look for the words "Invoice Number" for invoice document types and can look for the words "Mortgage Deed" for the deed document type. Systems such as Ephesoft can use the extraction results to find out where a document starts and ends. This process is known as **separation**. For example, Ephesoft can be configured to capture invoice numbers from every page of the scanned batch and separate documents only when the invoice number changes between pages so that multi-page invoices can be grouped together automatically.

- **Content analysis based classification**: This technique is used to classify documents by giving a few samples. Document capture systems learn the content of the document using a sample provided so that if documents with similar content are processed by the system in the future, they are classified accurately. In addition to classifying documents, one of the benefits of this technique is the ability to separate document boundaries.

- **User interface for exception handling**: No computer system or program is perfect. To make sure document capture systems do not produce mistakes, they provide exception handling queues or screens for the operators to ensure documents with lower confidence can be handled. Ephesoft provides a web-based user interface called **Document Review** where users are asked to look at documents that are marked by the Ephesoft system as "unconfident". By highlighting the exception documents, users can process the documents and batches with greater efficiency. It is important to note that these exception queues are designed to let users process more documents in a given time frame by utilizing keyboard shortcuts, search within document types, compare fields within the document, and apply custom validation scripts.

Extraction methods

Capture requirements often need to extract information from or associate information with the document before it is exported. The following methods are commonly used for extracting information from images:

- **Zonal OCR, ICR**, and **OMR**: These are techniques used to capture data fields from fixed forms. Handwritten zones and checkboxes can also be captured easily using this method.

- **Keywords** or **patterns**: This technique is used to capture information from semi-structured or unstructured forms such as invoices or letters. Capture systems can find patterns such as matching date formats or account numbers. In addition, capture systems can locate keyword(s) such as "Invoice Date" and capture the date next to this keyword rather than all the dates on the document.

- **Database matching**: This technique is used to match the incoming documents to database records. For example, an insurance company has database records for all its customers so it can automatically match incoming letters to a customer by searching words and numbers on the incoming document to their database. Ephesoft makes this configuration easy to implement.

- **Coordinate information**: Some metadata on the documents can only be captured by analyzing the coordinates of the values. The best example for this is when the system is processing tables or line items on documents. A bank statement or an invoice containing line items can only be captured by finding where each column resides in relation to other columns.

- **User interfaces for exception handling**: Similar to exception handling for classification results, document capture systems provide queues and screens to handle extraction results. Operators can look at the fields that are in question (unconfident, empty, or incorrect) and make the necessary corrections. Similar to Document Review, these validation or verification screens have several options to make the operator efficient. For example, validation screens allow the user to click on the words to enter in the field value without any typing. With this approach, an operator can capture pages with many line items with a few mouse clicks.

- **Communicating with outside systems**: It is important to note that document capture systems are designed to connect with outside systems in order to make sure the data being captured is accurate. For example, the "Purchase Order number" on an invoice or a "Customer Account number" in a correspondence may have to be validated with a backend database to ensure the accuracy during the extraction step. The system should flag any exceptions and present them to the operator using the exception handling user interface. To provide this functionality, many document capture systems, including Ephesoft, provide methods to connect with other systems interactively or in an automated fashion.

Export methods

Capture systems often have the need to push out classified and indexed documents to external systems for processing and archival. Common export methods include the following:

- **File system**: In its most basic format, document capture systems provide the information (electronic image files with the extracted metadata) in a file system folder or network share. Capture systems output electronic files in various formats such as PDF, TIFF, and metadata is generally stored in files such as XML, CSV, and so on.

- **Application Programming Interface (API)**: More advanced capture tools provide information using direct communication to backend systems such as repositories and workflow systems. A good example of this is the new standard for exchanging information between ECM systems called Content Management Interoperability Services (CMIS). Using CMIS, a document capture system can connect to repositories and export the data to them seamlessly.

What sets document capture apart from the other ECM tools?

The answer is hard ROI. Document capture is one of the few systems that can result in fast ROI by automating labor-intensive processes. Unlike other systems, such as workflow, repository, or web content management which may provide only soft ROI (better customer service, convenience, security for disasters), capture systems provide both hard and soft ROI that generate real money savings to an organization.

Document capture systems can automate many manual tasks, allowing companies to significantly increase their processing throughput. Some organizations see this as an opportunity to increase their volume using the same labor force. Other organizations see this as an opportunity to reduce their labor force or move them to other departments to save money.

Other benefits of document capture systems, including soft ROIs, can also be good reasons for a company to implement such systems. The power of these systems and their far-reaching benefits are constantly being explored. Here are a few examples:

- By automating mailroom operations, an insurance company can deliver the incoming mail to its departments electronically, classified and extracted, within hours instead of days. Claims or payments can be processed much faster, providing a strategic advantage over their competitors.

- By automating the sales order process, a manufacturer can ship and bill customers within minutes rather than days.

- By automating invoice extraction, a construction company can free up staff in its accounting department to focus on other tasks.

- By automating the records management department, a hospital can scan patient records in hours and make them available to doctors through online repositories grouped by patient and treatment.

- By automating the human resource function, an organization can be assured it has proper controls for sensitive employee forms and fast, accurate access to them.

Summary

Having read this far, you should now understand the basic concepts behind intelligent document capture. You should understand document classification and separation, and be familiar with different document classification techniques. You should also know how metadata can be extracted from the body of a document.

In the remainder of this book, we will look specifically at Ephesoft, starting with a tour of its basic features. The next chapter will discuss configuring Ephesoft to process your organization's documents. Following chapters will cover advanced topics such as integrating Ephesoft with your company's directory service (like AD or LDAP), customizing Ephesoft's appearance and behaviour, and exporting documents to any document management system that supports the industry-standard CMIS interface.

2
A Quick Tour of Ephesoft

Ephesoft has two user interfaces. One is intended for use by operators to review and validate Ephesoft's classification, separation, and extraction. The other is intended for use by system administrators in the configuration of Ephesoft. Not all aspects of Ephesoft can be configured through the administrative interface, however. For some of the configuration, administrators will need to use a text editor to modify files in Ephesoft's installation directory.

Before we begin, it is helpful to understand some commonly-used terms. A **batch** or a **batch instance** is a set of document images that are processed together. A **batch class** is a set of rules for processing a batch.

In this chapter, we will provide a brief introduction to Ephesoft's user interfaces:

- The administrative user interface
- The operator user interface

The administrative user interface

The administrative user interface has five tabs across the top that provide access to key areas of the system. They are as follows:

- Batch Class Management
- Batch Instance Management
- Workflow Management
- Folder Management
- Reports

Batch Class Management

The **Batch Class Management** interface allows administrators to create, modify, edit, and delete batch classes. The batch class configuration is broken down into sections for workflow modules and plugins, document types and fields, e-mail configuration, batch class fields, scanner profiles, and CMIS import.

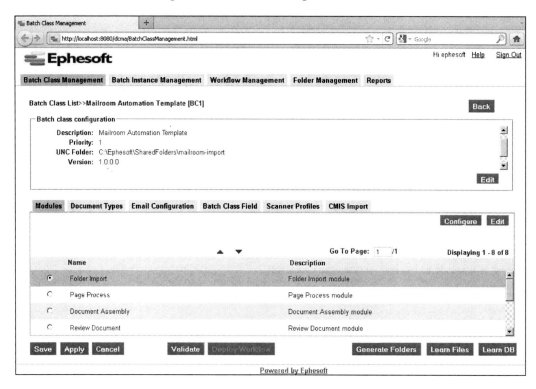

Administrators can configure six aspects of a batch class. They are as follows:

- **Modules** and **Plugins**: Modules are the major steps in the workflow. Each module is implemented by a series of plugins. An administrator can configure the plugins that comprise a module by selecting the module and pressing the **Edit** button.

- **Documents** and **Fields**: The **Document Types** tab is where the documents that will be processed in the batch class are specified. Fields can be specified per document. Extraction rules for automatic indexing of field values can be created as well.

- **Email Configuration**: Ephesoft can process e-mail messages and attachments. Ephesoft is configured with authentication information to check mail on an account, and it will process any e-mail sent to that account.

- **Batch Class Fields**: This prompts users for batch-level information from the **Web Scanner**. They can also be used in scripting to persist information at the batch level.

- **Scanner Profiles**: This is where administrators can configure Web scanners associated with each batch class.

- **CMIS Import**: Ephesoft can monitor documents in an existing document repository to import into Ephesoft for classification and extraction.

Batch Instance Management

Batch Instance Management within the administrative interface allows administrators to see the status of batches and restart in-flight workflows starting at a previous step in the workflow.

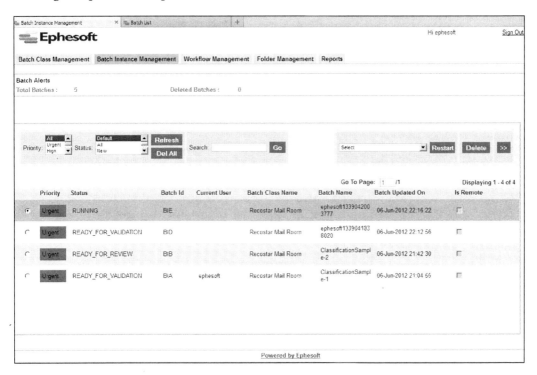

Workflow Management

The **Workflow Management** interface allows users to add new custom plugins and create dependencies. The following screenshot shows the **Workflow Management** interface:

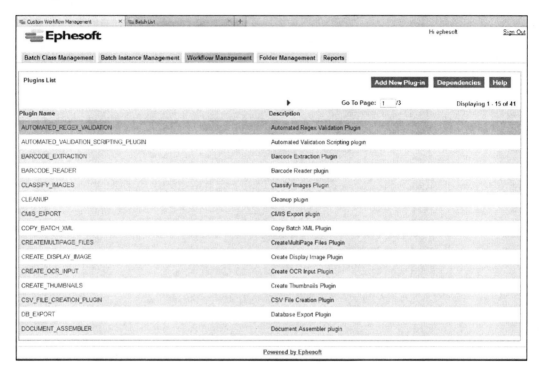

Ephesoft is designed to accommodate customizations to fit any customer's needs. For this reason, Ephesoft incorporates the jBPM workflow engine. This gives Ephesoft the ability to adapt to specific customer requirements from the capture workflow perspective.

Ephesoft's capture workflow can be thought of as *workflow within a workflow*. The workflow for each batch class consists of major steps called modules. The main modules that come with Ephesoft are the following:

- **Import**
- **Page Processing**
- **Document Assembly**
- **Document Review**

- **Extraction**
- **Document Validation**
- **Export**

Each module above is composed of a series of substeps called plugins. It is worth noting that some plugins may depend on other plugins. For example, the CMIS export plugin requires the `CreateMultiPage Files` plugin so that it can upload documents instead of individual pages.

Ephesoft allows developers to add custom modules and plugins to the Ephesoft capture workflow. The ability to add custom modules allows Ephesoft to extend to meet any document capture need. The ability to remove unused modules allows Ephesoft to run as efficiently as possible, maximizing the use of expensive server hardware.

Folder Management

The **Folder Management** interface allows the administrator to upload new and updated files for batch class creation.

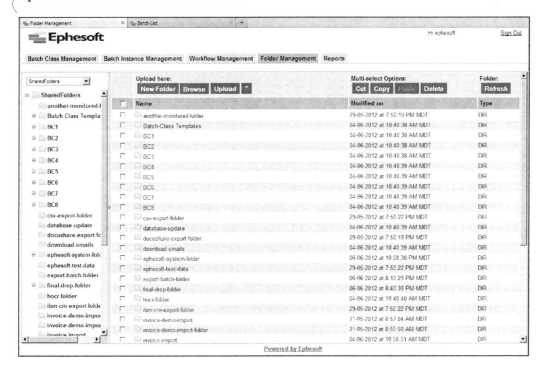

Reports

Reporting can be enabled to provide administrators with statistics on the average time batches, documents, and pages that are processed on each module or plugin. The administrator can filter by batch class, start and end date, and type of report.

To access reporting, click on the **Reports** tab in the administrative user interface.

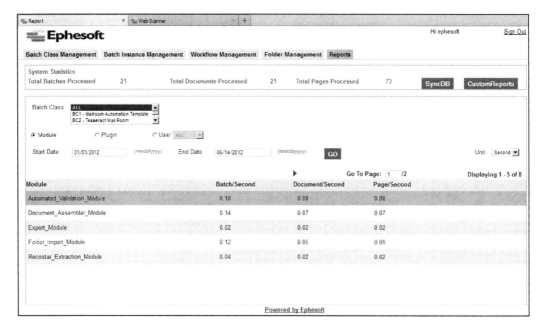

Operator user interface

The operator interface has tabs across the top that provide access to four key features:

- Home/Batch List
- Batch Details
- Web Scanner
- Batch Upload

Batch List

The operator's **Home** screen shows the batches that are in the review and validation steps and allows the user to select batches to process.

The **Review** process involves documents that could not be classified with the trained confidence to a document type. Operators can split and merge pages of documents and specify the document type for each document.

The **Validation** process involves index fields that could not be extracted or where the index values do not comply with the validation patterns specified for the field.

Batch Detail

The **Batch Detail** screen presents the operator with the next available batch for processing according to priority and batch date.

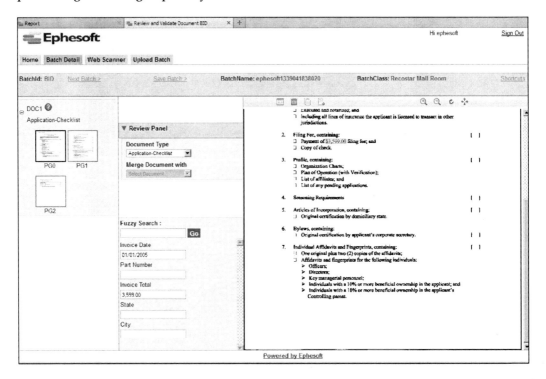

Web Scanner

The **Web Scanner** feature uses a Java applet to enable the operator to send content directly to the server from any TWAIN-enabled scanner.

The first time a user logs into the operator interface and selects the **Web Scanner** tab, the user will have to choose a scanner. When the user selects the **Select Source** button, the user will be shown all TWAIN devices that have been installed on the machine. Once the scanner is selected the user can select the appropriate batch class and start the scan job. Once the scanning is complete, the user is able to press **Stop** then the **Finish** button to start the batch processing.

The **Web Scanner** will scan directly to the server. Depending on the size of batch and bandwidth of the network you may want to consider using a desktop capture tool that submits jobs to Ephesoft via the monitored folders.

Upload Batch

Operators can submit PDF and TIF files directly to Ephesoft for processing using the **Upload Batch** feature. Once documents are selected and uploaded the operator can select the appropriate batch class and start the batch processing.

File system

The following are some important directories that are created when Ephesoft is installed. These are subdirectories beneath the Ephesoft installation directory:

- Apache 2.2: Apache can be used in front of Ephesoft for load balancing and failover. It is included in the installation but not configured.
- Application: The Ephesoft web application is installed in this directory.
- Application/i18n, images, css: These directories contain files to customize and localize the Ephesoft application.
- Application/native/RecostarPlugin: This plugin provides the image OCR functionality.

- `Application/native/Tesseract-OCR`: This plugin provides the image OCR functionality using the Tesseract engine.

- `Dependencies/gs, ImageMagick`: Applications which Ephesoft uses for image manipulation are installed here.

- `Dependencies/licence-util, licensing`: These directories contain tools to collect information needed to generate and install license keys.

- `Dependencies/luke`: Luke is a tool that helps troubleshoot problems with Lucene indexes.

- `JavaAppServer`: This directory contains the Tomcat configuration for Ephesoft.

- `JavaAppServer/conf/catalina/localhost`: This is where the *contexts* are defined for Ephesoft; it is where URLs are bound to java code.

- `WEB-INF/classes/META-INF`: System configuration property files are stored in this directory.

- `Report`: The configuration for the automated updating of reporting data is stored here.

UNC Folder:

- `SharedFolders/BC99`: The configuration for each batch class is stored here. The contents of the batch class folder can be modified through the **Folder Management** interface by a batch class or system administrator.

  - `CMIS-plugin-mapping`: This folder contains the properties file for the mapping between the document fields in Ephesoft to the CMIS endpoint content model.

   A reminder that the Batch Class Administration allows you to create document field names with spaces in the name. Names with a whitespace do not work if you are using CMIS export.

  - `Fuzzydb-index`
  - `Image-classification-sample`
  - `Learn-index`
  - `Lucene-search-classification-samples`
  - `Recostar-extraction`
  - `Scripts`
  - `Test-extraction`
  - `Test-table`

- `SharedFolders/final-drop-folder`: Processed batches are placed in this folder pending export to another system.

 Any contents in the `SharedFolders` folder can be modified through the **Folder Management** interface by a system administrator.

Summary

In this chapter, we looked at the administrative user's interface and the operator's interface to Ephesoft. We also looked at the installation directory on the file system. Now it's time to put Ephesoft to work; in the next chapter you will learn how to train the system to recognize your documents and extract content from them.

3

Creating a Batch Class

A **batch class** is the definition of how Ephesoft processes a set of documents (a *batch*). You can have many batch classes defined with each batch class monitoring different sources for incoming content. When Ephesoft discovers a set of documents, it will create a new **batch instance** and associate that batch instance with a batch class based on the originating drop folder, scanner, or e-mail account.

Throughout this chapter we will walk you through the following topics:

- Copying an existing batch class
- Creating new document types
- Training the system for classification and separation
- Creating fields
- Setting up basic Key/Value extraction
- Regular expression listing
- Exporting

Copying an existing batch class

The batch classes that come with Ephesoft provide the core behavior that most organizations will need. An existing batch class can be modified for a new workflow, but we recommend making a copy of a batch class and using that as a base for the new batch class. Creating a copy maintains the original template batch class for use in creating future batch classes.

In this section, we will create a new mailroom batch class based on the **MailroomAutomationTemplate** batch class. We use this batch class as a template because it comes pre-configured with all of Ephesoft's functionality (although some of it is disabled). To copy the **MailroomAutomationTemplate** batch class, first select it from the list in the **Batch Class Management** tab of the administrative interface and then press the **Copy** button above the list and to the right as shown in the following screenshot:

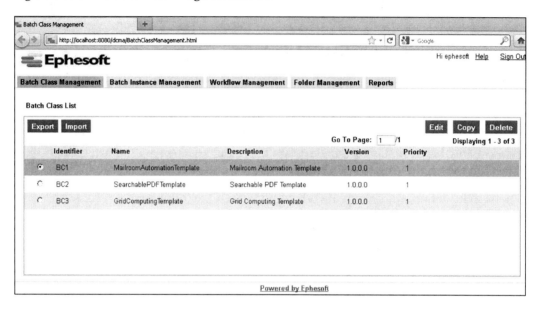

Enter the **Name**, **Description**, **Priority**, and **UNC folder** for the new batch class. The **Name** must not contain spaces or hyphens. The **Priority** can be a value from 1 to 100 with one being the most urgent. Instances of this batch class will inherit this priority, and processing of higher-priority instances will take precedence over lower-priority instances. The **UNC folder** can be a UNC path or local path and will be created automatically. The batch class creation will fail if another batch class uses this path. Ephesoft will monitor this folder for scanned content. When content is found, Ephesoft will create a new batch instance, applying this batch class' workflow to the documents it finds.

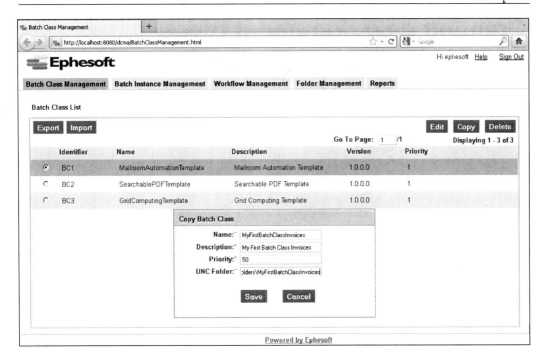

The new batch class will appear in the **Batch Class Management** tab of the administrative interface.

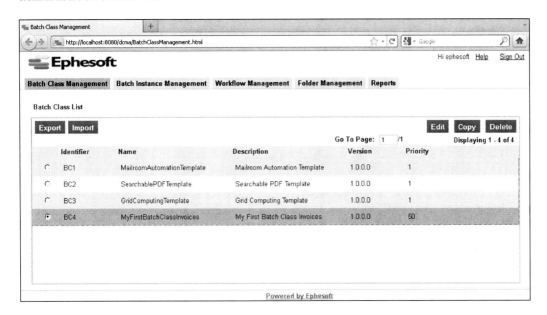

Creating new document types

Ephesoft uses document types to perform separation, classification, and extraction. Select the newly created batch class and press the **Edit** button or double-click on the batch class.

 Throughout Ephesoft's user interface, a list item can be edited by double-clicking on it.

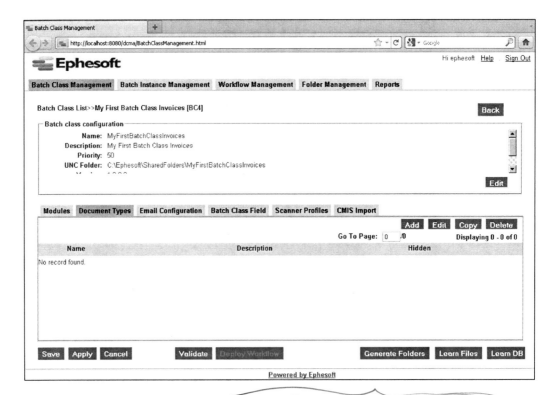

To create a new document type, press the **Add** button in the **Document Types** tab of the batch class. This will open the **Document Type configuration** interface for a new document type.

When confirmation dialogs appear, such as when you delete a document type, you can press the *return/enter* key rather than selecting the **OK** button with your mouse.

When you make a working change, such as deleting a set of document types or a working extraction rule, press the **Apply** button to save the changes. You can also press **Save**, but this will redirect you back to the batch class management home page. If you navigate away from a page without saving or applying your work, your changes will be lost.

always

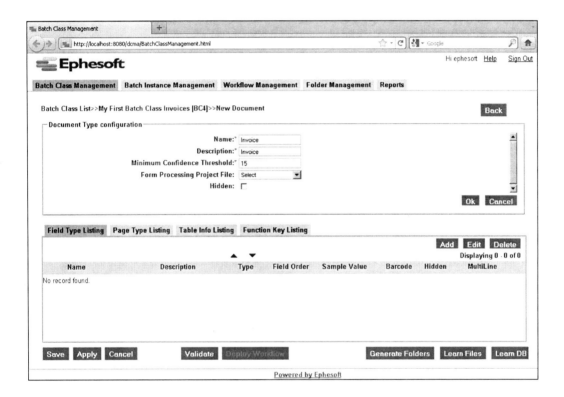

Next, enter the configuration information for the new document type. The name and the description should represent the type of document to be processed and should be easily understood by the Ephesoft operators. Both the name and description are usually displayed, but when you're configuring Ephesoft, you will use references to the batch class' name.

- **Name**: This will be the name of the new document type. This should be a short name. Ephesoft used to require that names be a single word, so you will often see batch classes named using *camel case* such as: "MyBatchClassName".

- **Description**: This is the description of the new document type. This can be the same as the name, or a more detailed description if desired.

- **Minimum Confidence Threshold**: This value ranges between 0 to 100. Ephesoft calculates a confidence using weights specified in the DOCUMENT_ASSEMBLER plugin within the Document Assembly module. This value indicates Ephesoft's certainty (or uncertainty) score that the page it is looking at is part of this document type. If Ephesoft's best guess is that the document is this document type, but the calculated confidence is below the document's minimum confidence threshold, then an operator will have to review this decision.

- **Form Processing Project File** (if applicable): The form processing project file is a RecoStar project file that can be used for processing fixed form information with handprint or checkboxes. Both KV extraction and RecoStar extraction can occur for a single document type.

Once this information is populated, press the **Ok** button in the **Document Type** configuration window then the **Apply** button.

System training for classification and separation

After the document type has been saved to the batch class, press the **Generate Folders** button from the **Document Type** configuration interface. This creates the folders on the server into which documents will be placed to train Ephesoft's classification engine. For this example, we will only train the system for search classification; the most common type of classification. Other types of classification will be discussed later.

The **Generate Folders** button will create folders in the following path:

```
C:\Ephesoft\SharedFolders\%BatchClassIdentifer%\lucene-search-
classification-sample\%DocumentTypeFolder%
```

Throughout this book, when specifying a folder path, we will use a convention similar to Windows environment variables, for example `%VAR%`. In the path above, the batch class identifier is referenced as `%BatchClassIdentifier%`. You will have to substitute the correct batch class identifier value, which is displayed in the administrative interface. The document type folder is referenced as `%DocumentTypeFolder%` and the value is set in the **Name** field of the document type configuration above. In this chapter's examples, the value of `%BatchClassIdentifier%` is BC4 and the value of `%DocumentTypeFolder%` is Invoice.

Also, examples in this book assume you have installed Ephesoft in the default location. If you've installed Ephesoft elsewhere, you will have to adjust your path.

As seen in the following illustration, the **Generate Folders** button creates the following folders:

- `SharedFolders/BC4/lucene-search-classification-sample/Invoice/ Invoice_First_Page`
- `SharedFolders/BC4/lucene-search-classification-sample/Invoice/ Invoice_Last_Page`
- `SharedFolders/BC4/lucene-search-classification-sample/Invoice/ Invoice_Middle_Page`

Using the **Folder Management** tab in the administrative interface, place documents to be used for training under these folders. The training document must be broken into pages and placed into the sub-folders for the first page, last page, and middle pages. If the training document has only one page, place it in the first page folder. If the document has two pages, place the first page in the first page folder and the second page in the last page folder. If the document has three or more pages, then all pages other than the first and last pages should go in the middle page folder.

Use the **Browse** button to select files from your computer, then click the **Open** button in the browse dialog. Next, click the **Upload** button to save the files to the selected folder on the Ephesoft server.

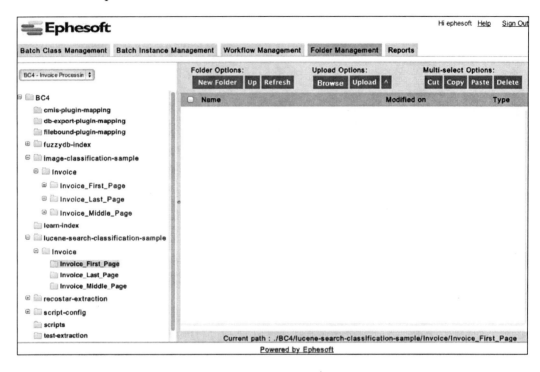

The **Generate Folders** button also creates folders that can be used to train Ephesoft for image classification; these can be seen in the previous illustration under the **image-classification-sample** folder. Image classification is discussed in *Chapter 6, Ephesoft Extended Features*.

Tools like IrfanView allow you to extract all the pages of multipage images and convert from PDF to TIF.

If you have documents that do not have a consistent last page you can place all the pages following the first page in the middle pages folder to get better classification confidence scores.

The most optimal way to train the system for separation and classification is to use blank forms if available. Later in this book, we will discuss how to optimize classification when no blank forms are available.

After the pages of the sample document have been placed in the appropriate folders under the **lucene-search-classification-sample** folder, press the **Learn Files** button. Ephesoft will then OCR the documents and create a Lucene index for the batch class. You will see a dialog when the index is successfully created.

Classification and separation can now be tested by using the **Upload Batch** user interface tab in Ephesoft's operator interface. Press the **Browse** button, select the files you would like to process and press the **Save** button.

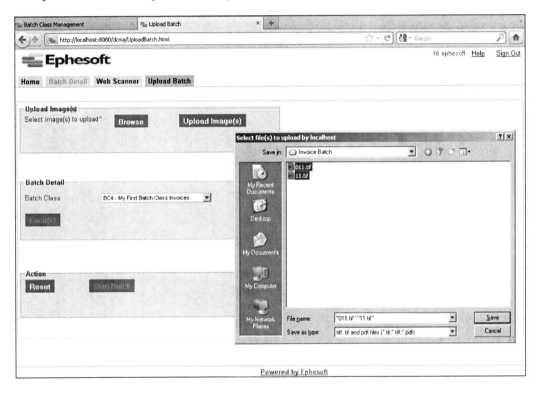

Press the **Upload Image(s)** button, select the **My First Batch Class Invoices** batch class and press the **Start Batch** button.

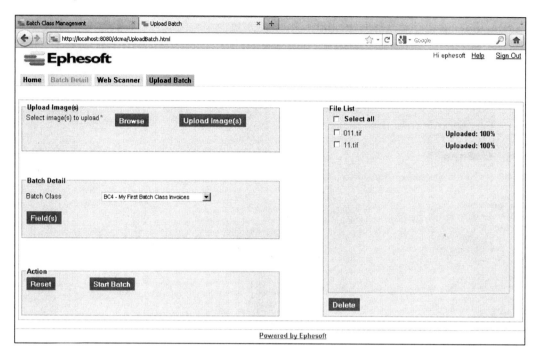

As Ephesoft processes the batch, the batch instance will have a **RUNNING** status visible in the **Batch Instance Management** tab of Ephesoft's administrative interface.

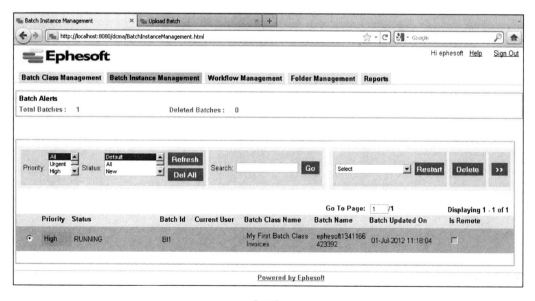

If the documents in the batch were scanned clearly and with sufficient resolution, then the textual content should be OCRed with high accuracy. Ephesoft will compare the text on each page in the batch with the text on the pages provided for training. If enough text matches, Ephesoft will classify the document as being of that type.

If Ephesoft's calculated confidence is below the minimum confidence threshold that was configured for the document type, then the operator will have to review the batch. Otherwise, the batch will run all the way through the workflow without any human interaction. Once the workflow is complete, the batch instance will disappear from the list on the administrative **Batch Instance Management** page.

The results of the batch processing can be found in the final drop folder here:

```
C:\Ephesoft\SharedFolders\final-drop-folder
```

Inside the final drop folder, Ephesoft will create a sub-folder for each batch instance. With minimal configuration, Ephesoft has performed two critical functions: separation and classification. If a single 99-page TIF file is fed into Ephesoft, the final drop folder might contain 33 three-page PDF files, each one a separate, complete document. This is **separation**.

Also, within the batch instance sub-folder is a file called `batch.xml`. This contains information about the document type that Ephesoft assigned to each PDF. This is **classification**.

The following is a portion of the `batch.xml` file where the document type is specified.

```
<Document>
  <Identifier>DOC1</Identifier>
  <Type>Invoice</Type>
```

Creating fields

Ephesoft stores information about a document in document level fields. Typically, field content is extracted from the document, but the fields can be populated in a number of other ways. The field content can be manually entered by the operator, for instance, or populated from a database, or calculated programmatically based on the values of other fields.

For the invoice document type, we would like to extract the customer number, invoice number, and invoice date. In order to accomplish this, we must first create the fields in the document type we created. From the **Batch Class Management** tab of the administrative interface, select and edit the batch class (**My First Batch Class Invoices**). From the **Document Types** tab, select and edit the Invoice document type.

In the **Edit** screen for the document type press the **Add** button in the **Field Type Listing** section.

Ephesoft will present a form requesting the following information:

- **Name**: This indicates the name of the field.

- **Description**: This indicates a description of the field. This is what is displayed to the operator.

- **Data Type**: Options include DATE, LONG, STRING, DOUBLE, INTEGER, FLOAT, BIGDECIMAL, and BOOLEAN.

- **Pattern**: Ephesoft will search the entire document for words that match this regular expression. This is useful when the data to be extracted has a distinctive format (such as a social security number), but may occur anywhere in the document. Regular expressions are required to be validated by clicking on the green check mark icon.

- **Field Order**: This is a number that Ephesoft uses to determine what order the fields are presented in the operator's interface.

- **Sample Value**: This is displayed in the operator's interface as a hint, indicating the valid format for data entry. A date field might say "mm/dd/yyyy".

- **Field Option Value List**: This allows the administrator to create a drop list of values from which the operator can select. A semicolon is used to delimit the values.

- **Barcode Type**: It is possible to encode field values in a barcode. This specifies what type of barcode is used to encode the value for this field.
- **Hidden**: Some fields may be used internally, and should never be presented to the operator. The administrator may indicate that such fields are *hidden*.

The **OK** and **Cancel** buttons are often hidden when this form is initially displayed. You may have to scroll down to find the **OK** button, which must be pressed to create the field.

The pattern is required, but not always useful. In cases where you have no use for a pattern, enter a string that is unlikely to appear in the document. We use **NOPATTERN** as a way of letting other administrators know that the pattern is not being used for extraction.

Ephesoft searches for words that match the specified pattern. Patterns that contain whitespace will never match anything, since Ephesoft is only comparing one word at a time.

Once all fields are created press the **Apply** button to save the progress (Or apply the changes after adding each field, if preferred).

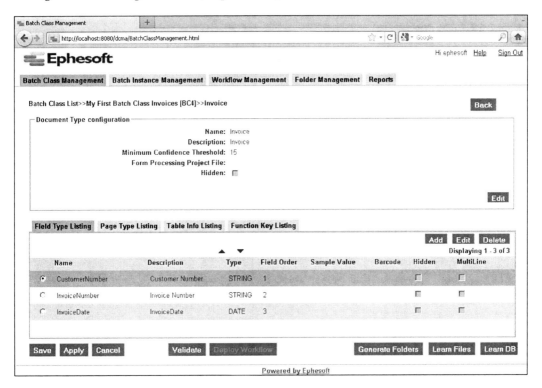

Basic Key/Value extraction

Next, Ephesoft needs to be configured to extract information from the document into the previously defined fields. One way to accomplish this is using **Key/Value (KV) extraction**. KV extraction works as follows: the administrator gives Ephesoft a *key* to search for on the page. This is often a field label on a form. Then the administrator tells Ephesoft to look adjacent to the field for content (the *value*) in a certain format.

> To use basic KV extraction, the value must be adjacent to the key. This technique works especially well with values either right or left of the key. If the value is not adjacent to the key, use the advanced KV rules, described later.

All the information to be extracted is in the upper-right section of the following document:

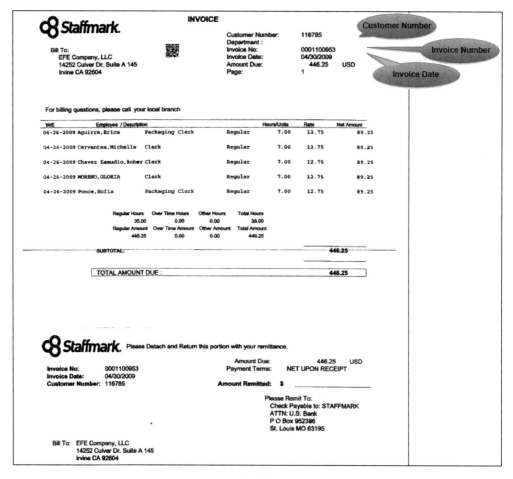

To define a KV extraction rule, select the desired field from the **Field Type Listing** within the **Document Type Configuration** interface and press **Edit**. The bottom half of the screen contains a tab for **Key Value Fields Listing**. Press the **Add** button to define a new KV extraction rule. Ephesoft will display a dialog box requesting the following information:

- **Key Pattern**: A regular expression that can be used to find the key.
- **Value Pattern**: A regular expression that defines the format of the content to extract.
- **Location**: The position of the value, relative to the key.
- **No of Words**: The number of additional words you would like to extract, following the value. The default value is **0** which means it will only extract a single word or string.

To collect the customer ID, a key pattern of `Number` and a value pattern of `\d{6}` is used. The invoice number could be collected using `No` and `\d+`, and the invoice date could use `Date` and `\d{2}/\d{2}/\d{4}`. The location for all three KV extraction rules would be `RIGHT`.

 Patterns are defined using Java regular expressions, the reference for which is found on Oracle's website.

 The best practice for defining key patterns is to use the smallest possible key pattern. This reduces the chance of OCR errors resulting in failure to match the key pattern. This is why we chose `Number` as the key pattern instead of `Customer Number`.

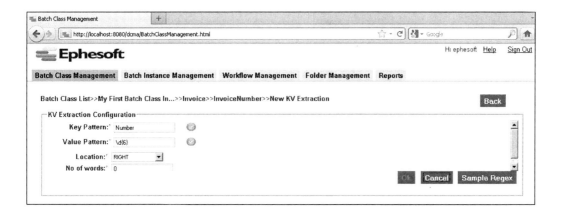

To test the extraction rules, place samples in the batch class' `test extraction` folder:

`Shared Folders/%BatchClassIdentifier%/test-extraction`

After putting the sample documents in this folder, press the **Test KV** button. This will OCR all documents in the `test-extraction` folder and then extract values that match the selected rule.

KV Extraction Result			
Close			
Page Name	**Value**	**Confidence Score**	**Coordinates**
011-0000.html	116785	100	{606,2447} , {732,2476}
011-0000.html	116785	100	{1865,270} , {1993,300}
11-0000.html	819349	75	{1647,2515} , {1838,2545}

The patterns entered for the rule may need to be adjusted in order for it to work properly. Once the rule is working as expected, press the **Apply** button to save the rule. After all extraction rules have been created, submit a batch to verify the rules are working as desired. Depending on the regular expression listings you have configured (this is covered in the next section), the document may stop in the validation state or simply be exported to the final batch folder where the batch XML file can be opened to view the extracted values.

Regular expression listing

Sometimes content will need to be adjusted or corrected for consistency before being saved. For example, it may be important to save all dates in the same format, even though they are provided in a variety of formats on the documents. Ephesoft accomplishes this with validation patterns that can be set on a field level. If the field's extracted value doesn't match the pattern, Ephesoft will force the operator to edit the field to conform. This ensures that values that have a pattern, such as dates and order numbers, will be validated prior to being exported.

To create a validation rule and edit the desired field, select the **Regular Expression Listing** tab and press the **Add** button. Enter the validation pattern then press the **Ok** button. Then press the **Back** button and save your changes by pressing the **Apply** button.

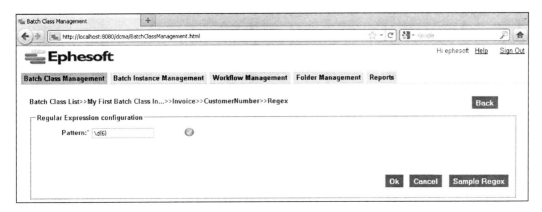

Export

Most organizations need to send their documents from Ephesoft to some other system. This is the final step in the mailroom workflow that we used as a template.

Ephesoft comes with several plugins available for exporting purposes. Some plugins are of general use, such as the CSV plugin or the Tabbed PDF plugin, while others are targeted at specific ECM products, such as the IBM CM plugin and the FileBound export plugin. There is also a CMIS plugin that allows export to any repository that supports version 1.0 of this industry standard interoperability interface.

More than one plugin can be active for each batch class, allowing you to export to multiple locations or systems. If no export plugin (or combination of plugins) meets your needs, it is possible to implement your own export plugin.

The only export plugin that is turned on by default is the Copy Batch XML plugin.

Copy Batch XML

The export plugin copies the processed documents to a location on the Ephesoft server's file system. An XML file is placed alongside the documents. This XML file contains the extracted fields and tables for each document as well as information about the batch.

By default, this plugin is enabled, and copies files to `C:\Ephesoft\SharedFiles\final-drop-folder`. If you want to disable the plugin, or if you want to change the drop location, you can edit the plugin configuration. From the administrative interface, select and edit your batch class, the export module, and then the **Copy Batch XML** plugin.

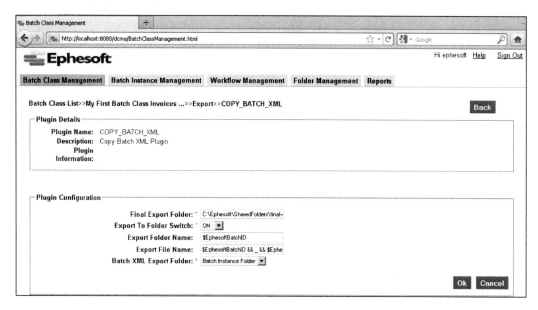

The plugin configuration will ask you to identify the following:

- **Final Export Folder**: This is the base export folder.

- **Export to Folder Switch**: This enables or disables the Copy Batch XML plugin.

- **Export Folder Name**: This is a variable name for the folder created for the batch in the final export folder. You can use generic variables, which are `EphesoftBatchID` or `EphesoftDOCID`. You can also use field names. `&&` should be used to concatenate different static values or variables. `$` should be used before variable names.

- **Export File Name**: This is a variable name for the document. You can use generic variables, which are `EphesoftBatchID` and `EphesoftDOCID`. You can also use field names.

- **Batch XML Export Folder**: Select **Batch Instance Folder** to place XML in the batch folder. Select **Final Export Folder** to place XML directly under the final export folder.

Summary

You've now learned the basics of how to configure Ephesoft. You can create a new batch class by copying one of the templates, you can train Ephesoft to recognize your document types, extract content into fields, and you can configure Ephesoft to export your documents and associated metadata into your content management system. In the next chapter, we will run a batch of documents through Ephesoft and learn to use the operator's interface.

4
Processing a Batch

Now that we have defined our batch class and trained it to classify documents and extract data, it's time to test it out. To do this, we will turn our attention to the operator's interface to process a batch. To process a batch, we will walk you through the following areas:

- Starting a batch
- Reviewing documents
- Verifying the extracted content

Starting a batch

First you'll need to find some test content. If your test content is a hard copy and you have a TWAIN-compatible scanner connected to your computer, you can scan images directly to Ephesoft using the **Web Scanner** feature of the operator's interface. If you already have page images, you can upload the images to Ephesoft using the **Upload Batch** feature.

Ephesoft can be configured to periodically check an e-mail account for new e-mails. Those e-mails (and their attachments) will be processed as batches. We will show you how to configure Ephesoft to ingest content from an e-mail account later in this chapter.

Most commonly, content is scanned using a high-volume production scanner and written to a network-accessible storage device. When you defined your batch class in the previous chapter, you specified a file system path that should be monitored for new content. In production, this is often a UNC network file path to the location where the scanner writes page images.

When a new batch is detected, regardless of its source (e-mail, web scanner, upload, or drop folder), Ephesoft will create a **batch instance** for the processing of that batch. Each batch instance is assigned an identifier. The batch instance ID begins with the letters "BI" followed by a hexadecimal number.

For the most part, Ephesoft processes each batch without human intervention. Administrators can look at the **Batch Instance Management** section of the administrative interface to monitor Ephesoft's progress in processing a batch. There are, however, two places where an operator may need to assist Ephesoft.

The first place is in **Review**, where Ephesoft will ask an operator to confirm the document's classification and separation. This review will only be requested if Ephesoft's confidence is below the threshold that you configured for that document type. Ephesoft will skip the review step for a batch if the confidence is greater than the threshold for each document in the batch.

The other place where an operator may need to assist Ephesoft is in **Validation**, which occurs when a validation rule is violated. In the previous chapter, for instance, we set up a validation rule saying that a customer number must be six numeric digits. If the content extracted to the customer number field does not match that format, Ephesoft will require an operator to edit the field's value.

Let's take a quick look at the process of reviewing and validating batch instances using Ephesoft's operator interface.

Document review

Ephesoft's review feature allows operators to specify the document type, delete, rotate, merge, and split documents as well as duplicate pages in the batch. Ephesoft directs operators to review a batch when any document in that batch is below its minimum confidence threshold. Documents in the batch that were separated and classified with confidence levels below the threshold configured for that document's type will have a red question mark icon. Documents that meet or exceed their confidence threshold will have a green check mark. By default, if all documents are recognized and the confidence is above the minimum confidence threshold, then the review step is skipped for the batch.

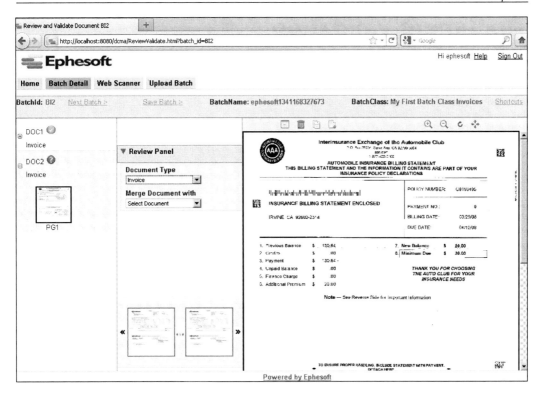

The operator can use keyboard shortcuts to merge a document with the preceding document (*Ctrl + /*), split a document into two documents (*Ctrl + T*), rotate a page (*Ctrl + R*), and so on. When the operator would like to save the progress of the batch, they can save it by pressing *Ctrl + Q* or *Ctrl + S*. All shortcuts can be found by clicking the **Shortcuts** link.

By saving with *Ctrl + Q* the batch will be saved to memory and every fifth save will be written to disk. By saving with *Ctrl + S*, the batch is saved to disk. *Ctrl + Q* is less time consuming and may want to be used especially with large batches consisting of many pages.

Ctrl + 0 provides instance search functionality to find the document type. This feature is very useful if there are hundreds of document types or many document types with similar names.

Document validation

Validation is the process of verifying extracted content. Ephesoft directs operators to validate a batch if any field of any document could not be extracted or if that field's validation rule failed. When an operator validates a batch, Ephesoft displays the first document that does not have all the valid values. Fields that require a value, or that with a regular expression validation pattern, will have a pink background color on the field if the value doesn't match the validation pattern. Validation cannot be completed if there are values not matching their field's validation pattern.

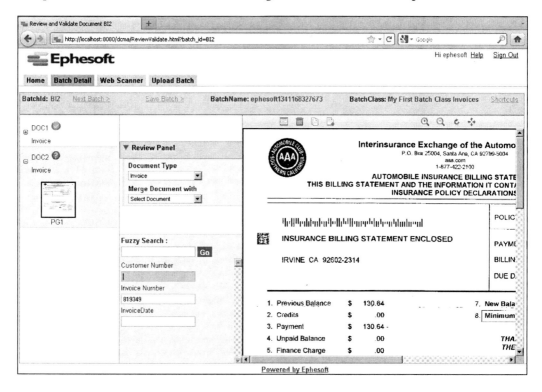

The field values can either be manually entered or a value can be extracted from the preview by clicking on it. Multiple words can be selected by holding down the *Ctrl* key and clicking on the values with the mouse. An area of the document can be selected by right-clicking on the top left-hand side corner of the area then dragging to the bottom right-hand side corner and right-clicking once again.

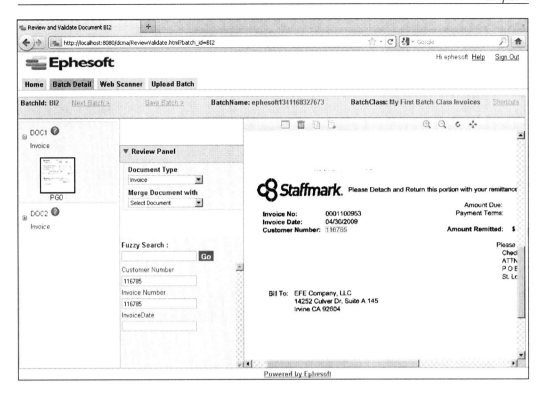

Documents in the batch that do not have all required values in the appropriate format will have a red question mark icon and documents that have all valid values will have a green check mark.

Once all of the values are entered, or extracted, for all documents in the batch, the user can save (*Ctrl + Q* or *Ctrl + S*) each document's field values. When the user saves the field values for the last document needing validation, they will receive a dialog indicating the batch is complete.

Summary

Congratulations! You're now familiar with the basics of Ephesoft. You know how to use the Ephesoft administrative interface to define how batches should be processed, and how to use the operator interface (when necessary) to help Ephesoft process a batch instance. You're far from done, however. In the next chapter, you will learn to use features that will allow you to more accurately classify documents, extract more content, and export to different destinations.

5

Core Ephesoft Features

You have now seen and used most of the basic features of Ephesoft. We have shown you the administrative interface, used it to create a batch class and to configure classification, separation, and extraction. We have also shown you how to use the operator's interface to process a batch instance, both in review and in validation.

doc. type   *extraction*

In this chapter you will learn the following:

- Different classification types
- New ways to extract content
- Other techniques for exporting your documents and metadata

Classification

In *Chapter 3, Creating a Batch Class*, we showed you how to configure Ephesoft to recognize an invoice document. We used Ephesoft's default configuration (search classification), but there are several other configurations available.

Classification types

You can select the process Ephesoft will use to classify documents by editing your batch class, editing the `Document Assembly` module, editing the `Document Assembler` plugin module within that module, and then selecting a value for DA classification type.

The options available to you include:

Search

Search classification (sometimes called **Lucene classification**) is the default classification method and is recommended for most content. When configured to perform search classification, Ephesoft compares the text on each input page to the text on training documents to determine its confidence that a document is of a certain type.

Image

Image classification is best used when classification cannot be made based on the content. This occurs on forms that do not have a lot of text, or where the textual content is unpredictable but the physical appearance, such as layout, graphics, and formatting, is consistent. Credit card applications that are *red dropout forms* (that is, where only the user-entered text is visible to the OCR engine) are candidates for this classification technique.

Barcodes

Barcodes can be used for documents that vary in content and layout, such as *white mail* (unformatted correspondence received in the mail). If a barcode is found on the page with a name that matches an Ephesoft document type, Ephesoft will set the current document's type to that type.

Automatic

The **automatic classification** type tells Ephesoft to perform all three types of classification. This may be necessary when no single classification technique will suffice for your batch class, but it will have a negative impact on Ephesoft's performance. This method looks for the classification types in the following order: Barcode classification, Image classification, and Search classification.

Confidence

Ephesoft calculates a **confidence** score for each page in a batch. The page scores are used to classify and assemble the pages into documents. Ephesoft also uses these page scores to create an aggregate score for each document. That score is compared to the confidence threshold for each document type in the batch class definition. Any document that receives a confidence score below the minimum threshold will be flagged for review. A batch with one or more flagged documents will be placed in a review queue for an operator to modify pages in the document and/or specify the document type.

Confidence scores are calculated differently for each classification type.

Search classification

The default classification type is search classification. Search classification separates and classifies documents using a two-step process. The first step is to collect information about the pages. The `Search Classification` plugin of the `Page Processing` module performs this function. The second step is to separate documents and determine their type. This is the responsibility of the `Document Assembler` plugin.

1. The `Search Classification` plugin calculates initial page scores by comparing the text on the page to the text on the training documents. Multiple scores will be generated for each page as Ephesoft finds several matches from samples for any given page. The page scores are then adjusted using weighted values that can be modified in the administrative interface by editing the `Search Classification` plugin of the `Page Processing` module. Pages can be weighted based on the page type (first, middle, or last). By default, Ephesoft is configured to reduce the scores for middle and last pages by 10 percent and 20 percent respectively as the first pages are more important when it comes to separation of the documents. This effectively biases Ephesoft in favor of using a page to start a new document (over using it as the middle or last page of a document).

2. Using the page scores calculated in the previous step (and adjusted using the weighted values from the `Search Classification` plugin), Ephesoft calculates all possible document assemblies and selects the result with the highest score.

The score is calculated as follows: The scores of each page in the assembly are averaged. Ephesoft then adjusts the average using a multiplier in the `Document Assembler` plugin. You will notice, looking at the following plugin settings screenshot, that there are several multipliers available. If the assembly has a first and last page, for example, the **DA Rule first-last Page** multiplier will be chosen. An assembly with first, last, and middle pages will use the **DA Rule First-middle-last Page** multiplier.

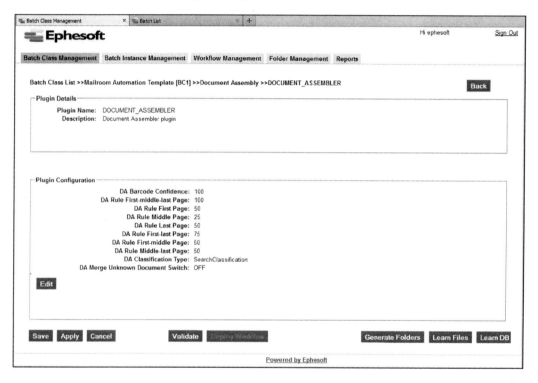

Suppose, for example, you have trained a batch class to recognize the first and middle pages of an invoice. If you run a three-page batch through Ephesoft, you might see results like this:

- Page 1 is determined to be the first page of an invoice because `Invoice_First_Page` received the highest score.

    ° Page 1 compared to `Invoice_First_Page` receives a score of 30.2

    ° Page 1 compared to `Invoice_Middle_Page` receives a score of 4.2

- Page 2 is determined to be the second page of an invoice because `Invoice_Middle_Page` received the highest score. Due to the order of this page in the batch, it's determined to be the second page of the invoice found in page 1.

  ○ Page 2 compared to `Invoice_First_Page` receives a score of 2.6

  ○ Page 2 compared to `Invoice_Middle_Page` receives a score of 12.2

- Page 3 is determined to be the first page of an invoice because `Invoice_First_Page` received the highest score. Since it is determined to be a first page it is a first page of a new document.

  ○ Page 3 compared to `Invoice_First_Page` receives a score of 31.6

  ○ Page 3 compared to `Invoice_Middle_Page` receives a score of 3.8

 In this case there is not a score for `Invoice_Last_Page` since there were no last page samples used to train this batch class.

The first document will have two pages: an invoice first page (page 1 of the batch instance) followed by an invoice middle page (page 2 of the batch instance). The second document will have one page as page 3 was determined to be the first page of an invoice. The confidence scores will be averaged to get the document confidence level:

- Document 1 (page 1 and 2): `(30.2 + 12.2)/2 = 21.2 x 50%=10.6`

  ○ Average score of pages, times weighed page

- Document 2 (page 3): `(31.6)/1=31.6 x 75%= 23.7`

  ○ Average score of pages, times weighed page

If the minimum confidence score for the invoice document type was set to `10` then this batch would skip the review step and move directly to extraction. If the minimum confidence score for the invoice document type was set to `20` then this batch would stop in review with the first document requiring review.

Barcode classification

Barcode classification is also a two-step process similar to search classification. In the Page Processing module, pages with barcodes are captured using one of two plugins, Recostar plugin or the Barcode plugin. In the Document Assembler plugin, Ephesoft creates a document when the first barcode is found and all the other pages are appended to the document until a new page with a barcode is found, creating the next document. The barcode value found by the barcode or the Recostar plugin must match one of the document type names.

Barcode classification is recommended when content classification cannot determine the difference between first, middle, and last pages. For example, multi-page invoices may have very similar content for the first and last page.

Image classification

Image classification is designed to work much like search classification. The Image Classification plugin collects page confidence scores. The Document Assembler plugin uses the image confidence scores to separate and classify documents. This is done using the same algorithm explained in the search classification section.

Automatic classification

Automatic classification can be selected to use all classification types. The scores from the various classification types will be added to come up with an aggregate score per page. That total value will be used for assembly and then classification scoring.

 SearchPdfClassification is created specifically for the SearchablePDFTemplate batch class type. This classification type should not be selected for the MailroomAutomationTemplate batch class type unless you want to merge all pages in a batch into one document with document type named "Searchable Document".

Programmatic classification

The document assembler script can be used with key/value extraction to classify and separate documents within a batch. This feature is best suited for documents where the classification and separation is based on the metadata on each page. For example, the key/value extraction at the Page Processing module can be configured to capture invoice numbers from every page of the batch and then the document assembler script can be programmed to separate and classify documents based on the invoice number.

Multiple layouts for a single document type

Often documents of a single type will vary widely in appearance. When this is the case, you can train Ephesoft to recognize all variations of the document as a single document type. This is accomplished by placing samples of each variation in that document's training folders. Then you'd configure extraction rules to tell Ephesoft how to find the metadata on each variation of the document.

 If you're using search classification and the text on each variation of the document is similar, you may only need to train one variation.

Let's configure Ephesoft to extend the Invoice document type established in *Chapter 3, Creating a Batch Class*. We have another invoice, as shown in the following screenshot, that looks quite different. The customer number on this invoice is misleadingly labeled as "policy number".

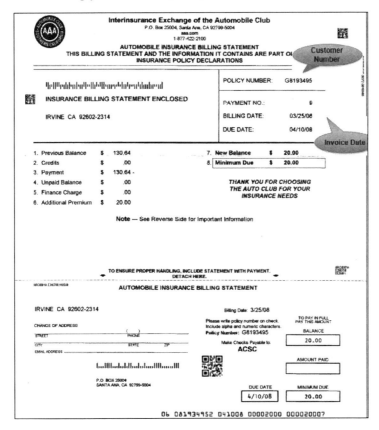

The new invoice format does not have the customer number as a 10-digit number to the right of the word **Number**. A new extraction rule must be created to obtain this value. In the **Key Value Fields Listing** for the customer number's field type, press the **Add** button to create a new extraction rule. Enter a key pattern of **NUMBER** and a value pattern of **G\d{7}** (to match the letter G followed by seven digits) and then press **Ok**:

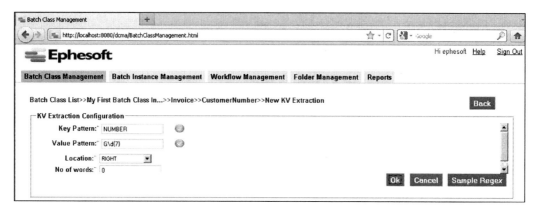

Press the **Back** button, select the new extraction rule and press the **Test KV** button. You should see your extracted content in a dialog box. If you do not see your extracted content you will need to adjust your rules. Once the extraction performs as desired, press the **Apply** or **Save** button:

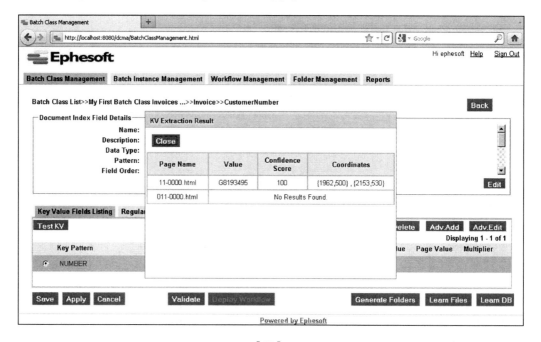

Once the extraction rules are created and tested for all the fields in this variation of the invoice document type, some samples should be run through Ephesoft to test all separation and extraction with multiple types of document types and formats.

Advanced KV extraction

When a value is not adjacent to a key pattern, Ephesoft's advanced KV extraction rules can be used to populate a field. This technique is also useful when a group of values need to be extracted from an area. Advanced KV extraction works very much like basic KV extraction, but instead of specifying the relative locations of the key and the value, a graphical tool is used to draw the regions on the page where Ephesoft should search for the key and the value.

Let's use advanced KV extraction to populate a field with the "Bill To" address from the invoice. First, create a field named **BillToAddress**, just as with basic KV extraction. Then, instead of pressing the **Add** button in the **Key Value Fields Listing** tab, press **Adv. Add**. Ephesoft will display a new screen for the creation of the extraction rule. Press the **Choose File** button and select a single-page TIF sample version of your document.

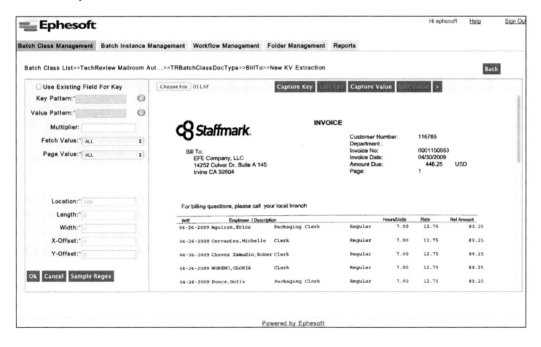

Enter the key pattern, just as with basic KV extraction. Then, select the regions for the key and value. Selecting regions in Ephesoft is a little counter-intuitive and is not done by click-and-drag. Instead, click and release at the upper-left boundary of the area to be selected. Then move the mouse to the lower-right boundary and click and release again. For this example, select a region around the words **Bill To** and then click the **Capture Key** button:

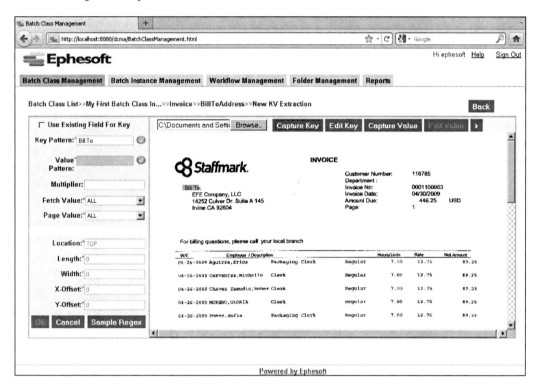

Enter the value pattern, then select the area around the address and press the **Capture Value** button.

 In the following example, we entered a value pattern of **.+** which will return any string with one or more characters.

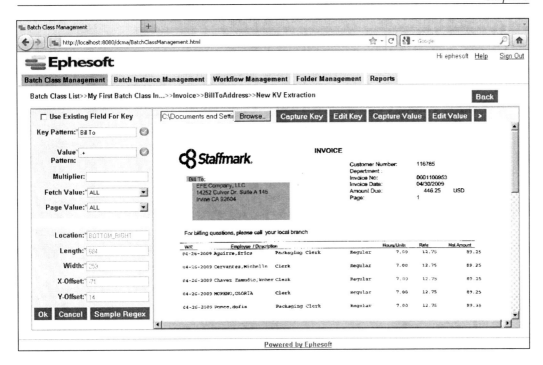

Press the **>** button and press the **Test Adv KV** button:

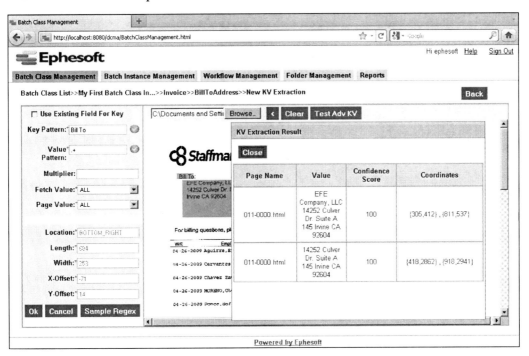

Fuzzy DB

When the "fuzzy database" is configured, Ephesoft can populate document fields with content from a row in an external database. Ephesoft automatically selects the row whose values match the most content in the current document. Ephesoft uses the Lucene full-text search engine to implement this feature.

> As of version 3.0, Ephesoft can also match an extracted field value to a column in a database.

Let's configure Ephesoft to populate fields on our invoice documents using information from a database. Assume that we have a database that contains vendor information, including the vendor's name and ID. This vendor ID differs from the customer number we extracted from the document. First, create the new fields of **VendorID** and **VendorName**.

> The database must contain a unique integer value that will be mapped to a `RowId` value in the Ephesoft configuration (discussed later in this section).

The following screenshot shows a database table containing vendor information:

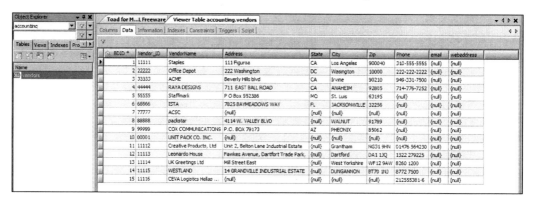

We need to configure the fuzzy database plugin to connect to this database. In the administrative interface, select **Batch Class Management**, edit the batch class, select the **Modules** tab, then select the **Extraction module** and press **Edit**.

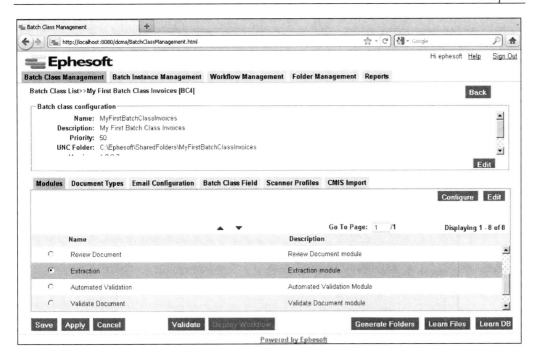

In the extraction module, select the **FUZZYDB** plugin and press **Edit**.

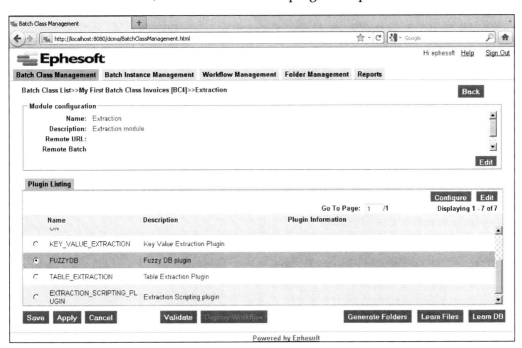

This displays the configured properties of the fuzzy database plugin. These settings can be modified by pressing the **Edit** button.

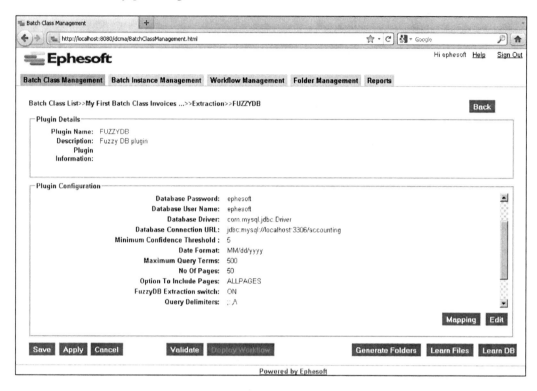

Enter the correct connection information for the database, specifically the username, password, database driver, and connection URL. Select **ON** for the **FuzzyDB Extraction switch** then press the **Ok** button. Don't forget to save the changes using the **Apply** button.

Ephesoft doesn't operate directly against the database. It uses a Lucene index that is generated from the database. Before using the fuzzy database feature, Ephesoft needs to be instructed to create this index by pressing the **Learn DB** button.

When your database content changes, you will need to update Ephesoft's Lucene indexes to reflect those changes. You can do this from the administrative interface by pressing the **Learn DB** button again or setting up automatic updating by configuring it in the `fuzzy-db.properties` file.

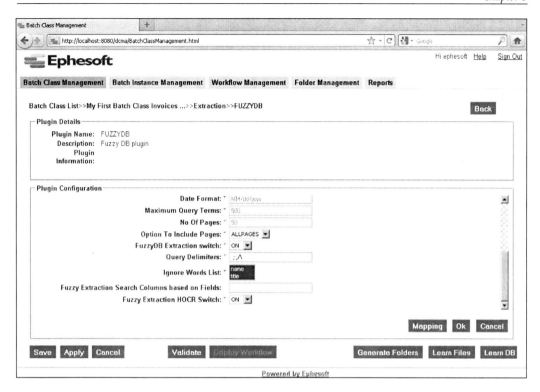

Next the Ephesoft fields need to be associated with database columns. Press the **Mapping** button at the bottom of the fuzzy database **Plugin Configuration** pane.

First, associate the Invoice document type in Ephesoft with the Vendor's table in the database. Select the table from the drop list and click on the **Map** button, as shown in the following screenshot:

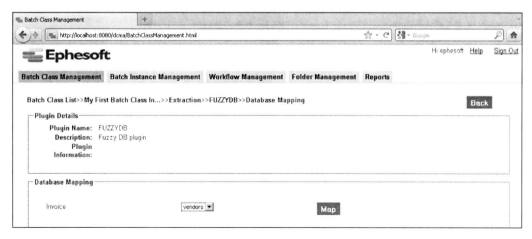

Now we can associate database columns with Ephesoft fields. First, choose a column to map to Ephesoft's hidden RowId field. We will use the primary key from our table, **BDID**.

 The fuzzy database feature requires that you provide a mapping for the RowId field.

Next, map the **Customer** field to the **VendorName** column and the **CustomerNumber** field to the **Vendor_ID** column. Press **Apply** to save your work.

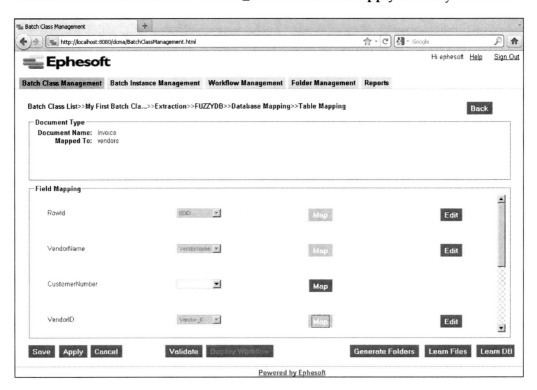

To test the fuzzy database, create a new batch that contains an invoice with information in the database. We are using one from *Staffmark*. In the following screenshot, notice that the customer number on the invoice is 116785, but that Ephesoft has extracted the customer number as **55555**. This is because Ephesoft found the vendor in the database named "Staffmark" and used that vendor's ID. Ephesoft uses the value from the database rather than the extracted value.

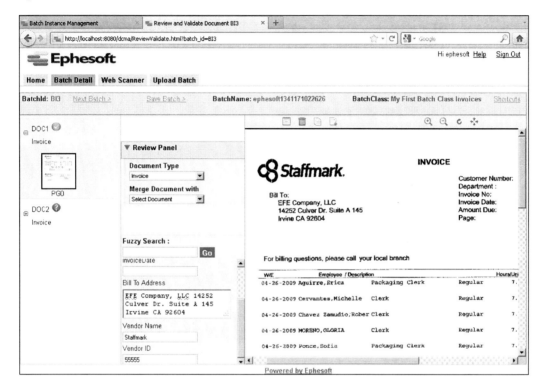

There is also an interactive interface to the fuzzy database feature. The operator can use this during validation by entering text to search for in the **Fuzzy Search** area on the page.

Ephesoft shows a list of database rows that contain the search term. Each row includes a confidence score; this score indicates how well the search term matched the row. When a row is selected, the mapped fields are populated with information from the database.

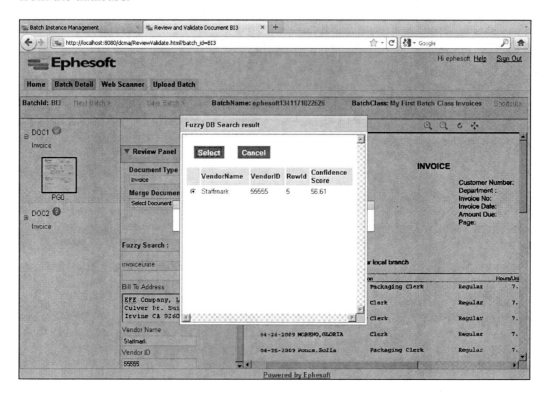

Using the Web Scanner

The Web Scanner can be used for sending documents directly to the server for processing. Users can scan using a TWAIN device or they can upload TIF and PDF images directly for processing.

The TWAIN driver and scanner must be set up before you can use the Web Scanner.

Because the images are sent directly on the server, bandwidth should be taken into account when using this feature.

The Web Scanner will not work from a Macintosh client.

In the operator user interface, select the **Web Scanner** tab, then press the **Select Scanner** button. Ephesoft will then display a security dialog. Check the **Always trust content from this publisher** box and press the **Run** button. Another dialog will pop up. Select the TWAIN device from this dialog and press **OK**. Then select the batch class workflow to run the scan through and press **Start**. The scanner will then start and images will be sent directly to Ephesoft.

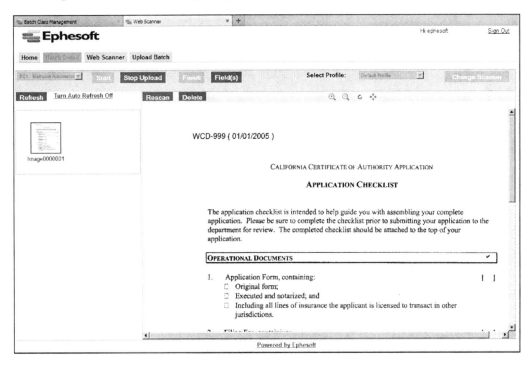

Scanner profiles can be created and edited on a per batch class basis in the **Scanner Profiles** tab under the Batch Class definition.

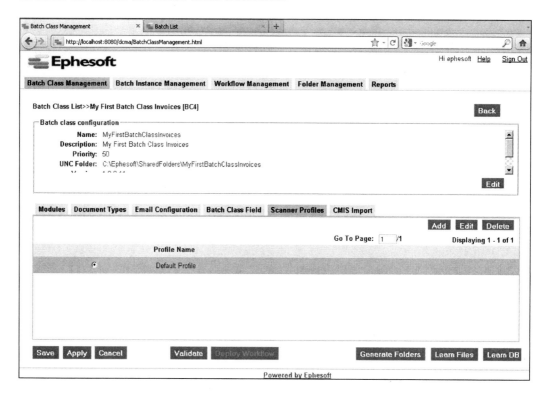

Uploading batches

The upload batch functionality allows an operator to select PDF and TIF images on their desktop and submit them directly to Ephesoft for processing. First select the **Upload Batch** tab and press the **Browse** button, then select files on the local machine.

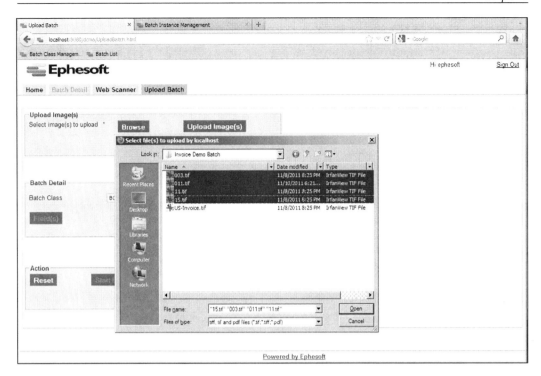

Once the images are selected and opened, press the **Upload Image(s)** button. Once the images are uploaded to the server, you will receive a confirmation dialog.

You can then select the appropriate batch class to process the images and press the **Start Batch** button to start the processing of the batch.

Export

In *Chapter 3, Creating a Batch Class*, we used the Copy Batch XML plugin to export content to the Ephesoft server's file system. There are a number of other options, however. The CMIS and JDBC export plugins use standards-based interfaces to allow you to export to a large number of enterprise content management systems and databases. Let's take a look at how to configure these two plugins, and then review the other plugins that are available.

CMIS Export

The **Content Management Interoperability Services (CMIS)** API is an open standard
for interacting with enterprise document repositories. You can use the CMIS Export
plugin to export your scanned content (and associated metadata) to any repository that
supports the CMIS standard, such as Alfresco, Documentum, FileNet, or SharePoint.
Let's look at how to configure the CMIS Export plugin to send content to Alfresco,
a popular open source enterprise content management system.

Establish a content model in your CMS

Suppose you have an invoice document type in Ephesoft that has fields for vendor
name, invoice date, and invoice total. The first thing you'll want to do is define
a custom content model in Alfresco to represent your scanned content. Alfresco
defines custom content models in XML files that look like this:

```
<type name="acme:invoice">
  <parent>cm:content</parent>
  <properties>
    <property name="acme:vendorName">
      <title>Vendor Name</title>
      <type>d:text</type>
      <mandatory enforced="false">false</mandatory>
      <index enabled="true">
        <atomic>true</atomic>
        <stored>false</stored>
        <tokenised>false</tokenised>
      </index>
    </property>
```

Alfresco document type and property name values have prefixes to prevent
namespace collisions in the content models. We have used a prefix, acme, in our
examples. The previous example shows a document type acme:invoice that
extends Alfresco's base document type (cm:content). This custom type has a
text property named acme:vendorName. Not shown are a date property named
acme:invoiceDate and a float property named acme:invoiceTotal.

Configure Ephesoft CMIS Export

Once you've got your content model set up, you'll need to configure Ephesoft to use
CMIS to send the processed content to Alfresco. There are actually three places in
Ephesoft where you need to configure CMIS export. They are as follows:

- The plugin settings in the administrative user interface

- The mapping file, in your batch class' `cmis-plugin-mapping` directory
- The global configuration file, located here: `C:\Ephesoft\Application\WEB-INF\classes\META-INF\dcma-cmis\dcma-cmis.properties`

Configure the CMIS Export plugin

From the administrative interface, go to the **Batch ClassManagement** tab and open your batch class. Navigate to the **Export** module and then to the `CMIS Export` plugin. This plugin comes configured by default with a disabled sample connection to Alfresco's public CMIS server.

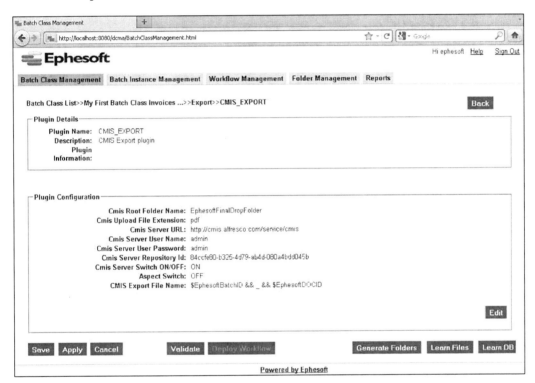

The CMIS plugin can be configured as follows:

- **CMIS Root Folder Name**: This is the name of the folder into which Ephesoft should load the exported documents. In Alfresco, this folder will be created underneath the root folder (which is typically named `Company Home`).

- **CMIS Upload File Extension**: This setting controls whether the documents are uploaded to your document management system as PDF or TIF images.

- **CMIS Server URL**: The services provided by CMIS are all defined in an XML *service document*; this is the location of that document. Alfresco 4.0 hosts this file at /alfresco/service/cmis.

- **CMIS User Name** and **Password**: The authentication information to be used to connect to the document management system.

- **CMIS Server Repository Id**: If a document management system is hosting multiple repositories, then each repository is listed in the service document with an associated identifier. You should examine the service document to find the identifier for your repository.

- **CMIS Server Switch**: This can be used to enable and disable exports to your document management system.

- **Aspect Switch**: This can be used to enable or disable support for aspects in an Alfresco repository.

- **CMIS Export File Name**: This allows you to create a pattern for renaming documents as they are written to the document management system.

Document type and property mapping

Next, you will need to associate Ephesoft document types with Alfresco document types. Ephesoft's fields also need to be mapped to properties of Alfresco documents. Edit the file: SharedFolders/BC123/cmis-plugin-mapping/DLF-Attribute-mapping.properties. This file contains some examples of content mapping. Delete the examples and set up your own mapping, like this:

```
Invoice=D:acme:invoice
Invoice.VendorName=acme:vendorName
Invoice.InvoiceDate=acme:invoiceDate
Invoice.InvoiceTotal=acme:invoiceTotal
```

The first line of this property file associates the document types, and the last three lines associate the fields. When mapping document types, you'll need to prepend a D: to the beginning of your CMS's type name. This is CMIS syntax for representing a document (as opposed to, for example, a folder).

Global CMIS configuration

The final area where CMIS can be configured in Ephesoft is this file: C:\Ephesoft\Application\WEB-INF\classes\META-INF\dcma-cmis\dcma-cmis.properties. This file affects the CMIS configuration of all batch classes.

The most commonly modified setting in this file is the date format. When you map a date field, Ephesoft needs to parse the date in order to reformat the information to match the CMIS specification. The `cmis.date_format` parameter specifies the expected date format. See the JavaDoc for the `SimpleDateFormat` class to learn how to specify date formats.

If your content management system uses **web service security (WSS)** to secure its CMIS web services, you will want to adjust the value of the `cmis.security.mode` property. This specifies the security mode to use when attempting to connect to the CMIS web services. There are two possible values: `basic` and `wssecurity`. HTTP Basic Authentication is the default setting for the Ephesoft CMIS connection. This corresponds to the basic setting for the `cmis.security.mode` property. The `cmis.security.mode` property is set to `wssecurity` in order to have the CMIS credentials that are configured in the **CMIS_EXPORT** plugin included in the `WS-Security SOAP` header of the CMIS web service requests.

If your CMIS web services are not addressable from a single URL, you can configure the location of each service used by Ephesoft. You'll see a set of properties that begin with `cmis.url`; these can be edited to specify where your content management system hosts that service's WSDL.

Database Export

DB Export allows document-level field values, metadata, to be exported to databases using JDBC. Administrators can map the document fields from Ephesoft to table columns in a database.

 The `DB_Export` plugin needs to be added to the workflow before it can be used. Please refer to the *Adding a Plugin to Ephesoft* section in *Chapter 6, Ephesoft Extended Features* on how to add a plugin to a module.

The Export plugin has two configuration points: the Batch Class plugin settings and the mapping file.

The Batch Class plugin can be configured with the following settings:

- Table name where the index fields will be exported
- Password
- User name
- JDBC driver name (this driver must be compatible with Hibernate)

- Database URL to allow plugin to connect to the desired database
- Switch to enable and disable `Export` plugin

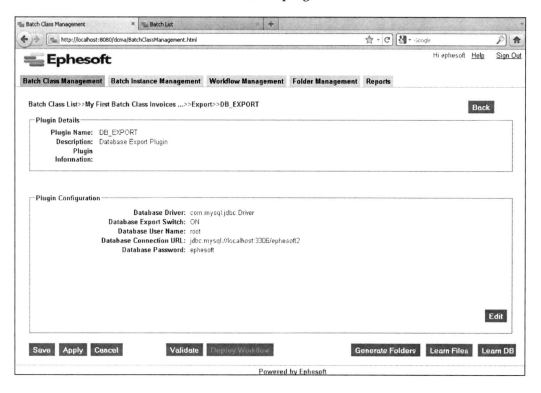

The mapping file designated for each batch class will allow administrators to map index fields to table columns. This file is located at `C:\Ephesoft\SharedFolders \%BatchClassIdentifier%\db-export-plugin-mapping\db-export-mapping. properties`. The following sample mapping file contains the location where index fields from an Ephesoft document type called Invoice will be mapped to columns in a database table named `InvoiceTable`.

`Invoice.type=InvoiceTable:invoiceType`

`Invoice.sender=InvoiceTable:invoiceSender`

`Invoice.receiver=InvoiceTable:invoiceReceiver`

`Invoice.total=InvoiceTable:invoiceTotal`

`Invoice.number=InvoiceTable:invoicenumber`

`Invoice.date=InvoiceTable:invoiceDate`

Other export plugins

So far, we have shown you how to export to the local file system or export using CMIS and JDBC. These are general-purpose plugins that can be used in a variety of situations. Ephesoft comes with other general-purpose plugins such as the csv plugin and the tabbed PDF plugin.

Ephesoft also provides plugins to facilitate export into specific content management systems, such as Docushare, Filebound, NSI, and IBM CM.

You can edit your batch class and then edit the export module to see the list of available export plugins.

Configuration management of batch classes

Batch classes can be exported from one Ephesoft server and imported into another. A new batch class can be created or an existing batch class overridden in the importing environment.

To export, select the batch class and press the **Export** button.

 Exporting can also be used to provide backup to the batch class to a code repository like Git or Subversion.

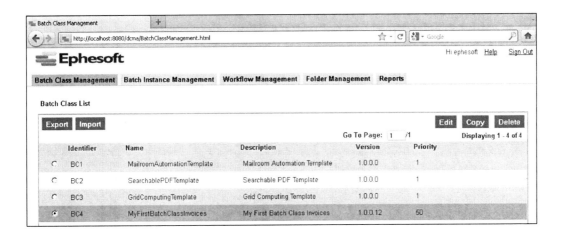

When prompted to select what options to export, select **All** and press the
Save button.

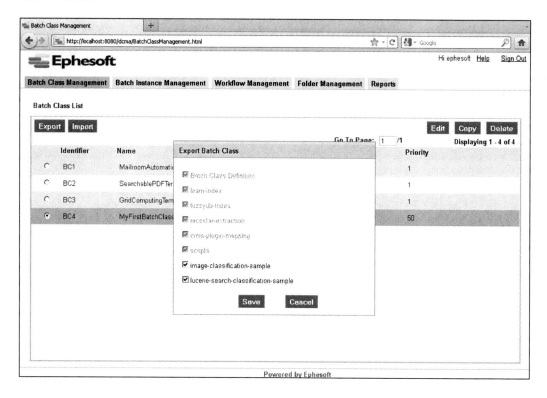

Save the exported batch class zipped file to your local machine.

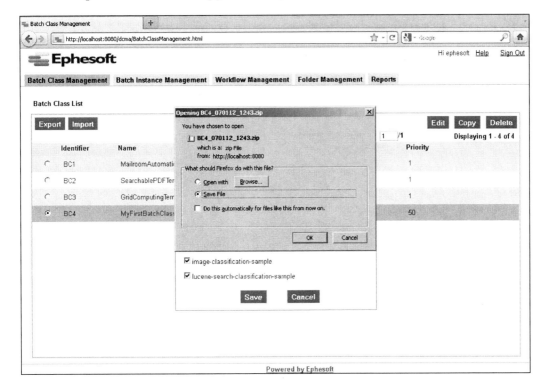

Next import the exported batch class into an Ephesoft instance. In the **Batch Class Management** screen, press the **Import** button.

Press the **Browse** button and select the exported batch class archive. Once the archive is selected, press the **Attach** button. To import a batch class for the first time, specify the **UNC Folder**, and select the **Roles**, **Email Accounts**, and **Batch Class Definition** checkboxes. Press the **Save** button to create the new batch class.

The **UNC Folder** value should be a full path.

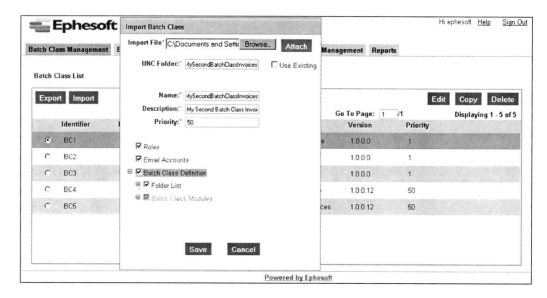

Once the new batch class is created it can be edited to set environment plugin information such as CMIS configuration, roles, e-mail configuration, and so on.

To override an existing batch class, select the **Import** button, attach the archive, and select the **Use Existing** checkbox. Select the correct **UNC Folder** from the drop-down of the batch class to be overridden.

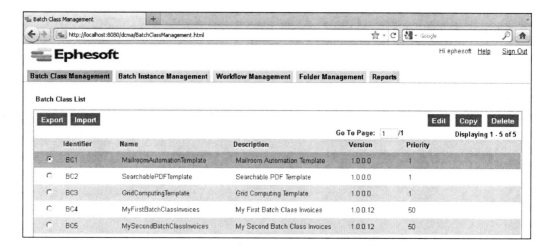

Select the **Batch Class Definition** checkbox then deselect the environment-specific items that should not be overridden. The typical settings that should not be overridden for import include:

- **Roles**
- **Email Accounts**
- **Batch Class Definition | Batch Class Modules | Export**

Press **Save** to override the batch class configuration.

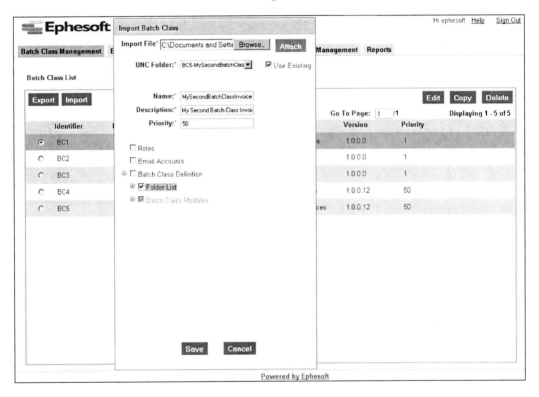

Summary

In this chapter, you have learned how to process forms with multiple different layouts, additional extraction techniques, the features that support database lookup, batch upload, web scanning, and much more. At this point, you should be able to use Ephesoft to implement intelligent document capture for a wide variety of organizations.

In the next chapter, we will cover advanced topics around Ephesoft's flexible framework such as scripting and custom workflows.

6

Ephesoft Extended Features

Now that you have a strong understanding of Ephesoft, we have saved a handful of advanced topics for last. Advanced topics are those that require the use of external applications (as is the case with RecoStar extraction), involve programming skills (as is needed in order to perform scripting), or are only used in special circumstances (such as grid computing).

Set aside a little extra time, and get ready to learn the details of Ephesoft implementation. The following advanced topics will be covered in this chapter:

- Other classification methods
- Additional extraction methods
- Scripting
- External application integration
- Workflow and plugin customizations
- Grid computing
- Automatic learning

Other classification methods

While search classification is the default and most commonly used classification type, there are other types that can be used instead of or in addition to search classification.

Barcode classification

Barcodes are useful for classifying documents that do not have a consistent format, such as correspondence mail. Using the classification type of BarcodeClassification or AutomaticClassification will utilize barcodes. This setting is in the `Document Assembler` plugin of the `Document Assembly` module. The barcode can be in any supported barcode format and should match the name of the document type exactly.

In the invoice example, we can create a QR code that has Invoice as the value.

If this code is found anywhere on a page, that page will be classified as a first page of an invoice document.

Ephesoft provides two mechanisms for locating barcodes. This feature is implemented in the `Barcode Reader` plugin and the `RecoStar` plugin. Both of these plugins are located in the `Page Process` module. If you want to perform barcode classification, we recommend that you use the `RecoStar` plugin. Leave the `Barcode Reader` plugin disabled as it comes configured by default, or remove this plugin entirely as described later in this chapter. Edit the `RecoStar` plugin configuration and turn on the barcode switch. The `RecoStar` plugin should already be enabled; the RecoStar switch is on by default.

Barcodes can also be used for determining separation of documents. To turn the feature on, select the `Document Assembler` plugin from the `Document Assembly` module. Set the value of **DA Merge Unknown Document Switch** to **ON**.

When you are using the `RecoStar` plugin, `FPR.rsp` needs to include a barcode field named `Barcode_1`. This is the default configuration for new installations but if you are upgrading Ephesoft, you may need to explicitly define this field using RecoStar Design Studio.

Image classification

It is possible to use images to train Ephesoft to classify and assemble documents. Using the classification type of ImageClassification or AutomaticClassification will enable this feature. As with search classification, you will need to provide samples of the document types. Ephesoft creates a thumbnail image for each sample page that is compared to the pages in the batch.

Documents used for training should be placed inside the following folder:

```
SharedFolders/%BatchClassIdentifer%/image-classification-sample
```

After the pages of the sample document have been placed in the appropriate folders under the `image-classification-sample` folder, press the **Learn Files** button. Ephesoft will create a thumbnail image for each sample. You will be notified when the images are processed.

RecoStar extraction

In *Chapter 3, Creating a Batch Class*, we created our batch class by copying the **MailroomAutomationTemplate** batch class. As a result, Ephesoft used RecoStar behind the scenes to recognize the text on scanned images. Up to this point, Ephesoft has been responsible for extracting content from the document into fields. Sometimes it is necessary to configure extraction inside RecoStar. RecoStar should be used if any of the following conditions apply:

- Handwritten content needs to be extracted.

- The form has checkboxes, and the state (whether the checkbox is checked or unchecked) needs to be extracted.

- The content to be extracted cannot be located relative to a key, and does not conform to a unique pattern. For example, the form might have an address in the upper right-hand side corner, but there is no label or header associated with this address.

You do not need to use just one technique; you can use RecoStar extraction, basic KV extraction, and advanced KV extraction all on the same document.

RecoStar extraction is only available in Ephesoft Enterprise for Windows.

Full page OCR is accomplished with a RecoStar project called `FPR.rsp` located in `SharedFolder/%BatchClassIdentifer%/recostar-extraction`. You may want to modify this project if you want to support languages (USA selected in the OOTB project) or modify the image manipulation or OCR settings. You can also create a new project to use for the OCR functionality. The project can be selected in the `RecoStar` plugin in the `Page Process` module.

Let us walk through the process of using RecoStar to extract a handwritten `Billing Code` field from an invoice. RecoStar extraction is not configured from within the Ephesoft administrative interface; instead, a Windows application called *RecoStar Design Studio* must be run. Ephesoft installed this at the following location:

```
C:\Ephesoft\Application\native\RecostarPlugin\
RecoStarDesignStudio\RecoStarDesignStudio.exe
```

Create a RecoStar project

Within RecoStar Design Studio, create a new project by selecting **New Project** from the **File** menu. Select the project type **Single Form** then press the **Next** button.

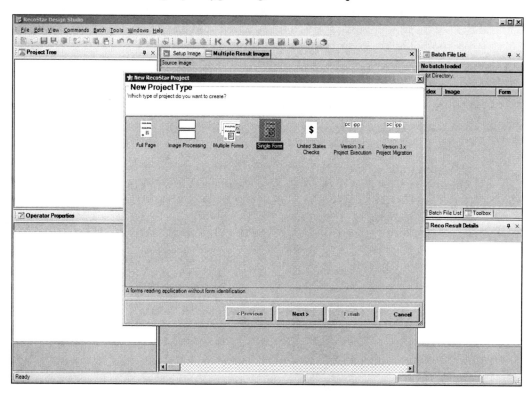

Enter a project name and location to save the file.

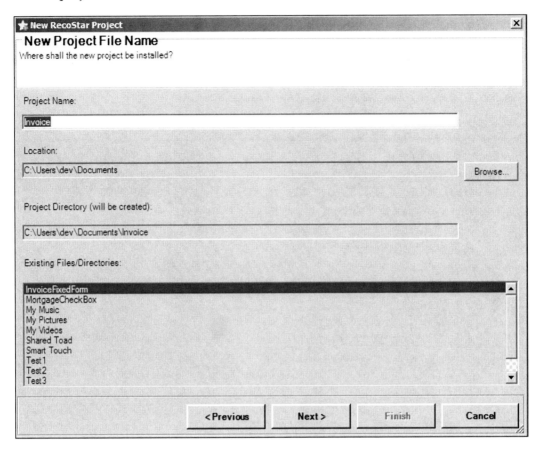

Use the **Add Files** button to select some working image files. Working image files are sample documents that RecoStar will use to test the configuration. Press **Next >** after uploading the working image files.

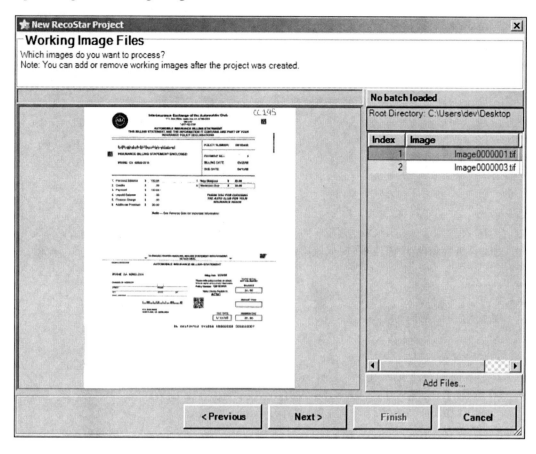

The next step in the RecoStar wizard for creating new projects is the **Mandatory Parameter** setup. Select the country/languages that appear on the documents to be processed.

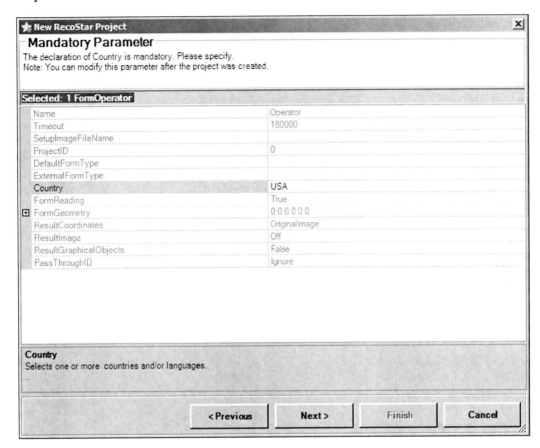

Finally, press the **Finish** button to create the project.

Configure the RecoStar project

The RecoStar form name must match the Ephesoft document type name. Find the default form in the **Project Tree** list and right-click on it. Select the **Rename** option and change the name from Default to Invoice.

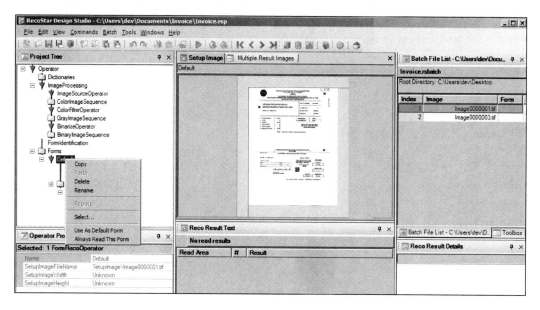

Configure a field to match an existing field in Ephesoft. In the **Project Tree** list, under the default form that we renamed to Invoice, there is a field named IcrField. Right-click on that field to rename it to BillingCode, matching the field name in Ephesoft.

Now we need to configure RecoStar to show where the customer name is located. Making sure the Customer field is selected in the **Project Tree** list, select the **SetupImage** tab in **DesignStudio**. Drag the red rectangle in the **SetupImage** tab so that it surrounds the top-right section of the invoice where the billing code is written.

Since the billing code contains both letters and numbers, we will turn off the LogicalContext flag.

There is a RecoStar tutorial available for Enterprise customers that explains more of these settings.

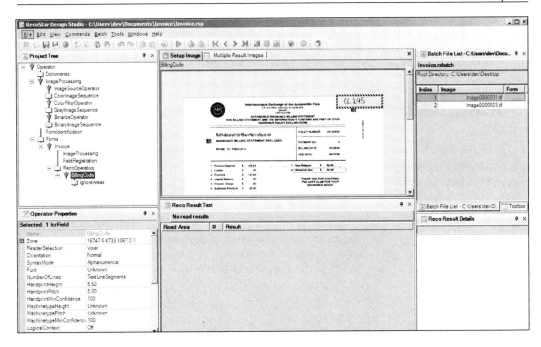

Press the **Play** button (the green triangle in the toolbar) to test out the extraction. The results will be displayed in the **Reco Result Text** area.

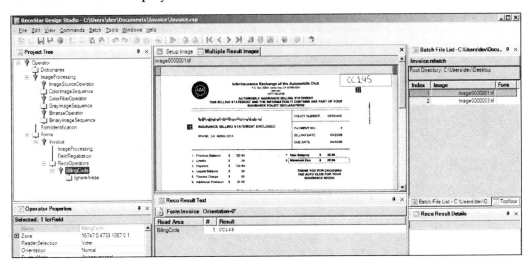

Once RecoStar extraction is tested and ready to be used in Ephesoft, save the project and copy the project file to the batch class `recostar-extraction` folder.

```
C:\Ephesoft\SharedFolders\%BatchClassIdentifer%\recostar-
extraction
```

RecoStar project files have an `.rsp` extension.

Configure Ephesoft to use the RecoStar project

The document type definition needs to be edited in order to use this RecoStar project. Go into the **Batch Class Management** tab of the administrative interface, and edit the **Invoice** document type. The new RecoStar project file should now appear in the **Form Processing Project File** drop list. Select the project file and create a new string `BillingCode` field. Click on **OK** and then click on **Apply** to save changes.

 Don't forget to verify that your document type name matches the RecoStar form name, and that your field name matches the RecoStar field name.

You must also turn on the RecoStar Extraction switch in the `RecoStar Extraction` plugin of the `Extraction` module.

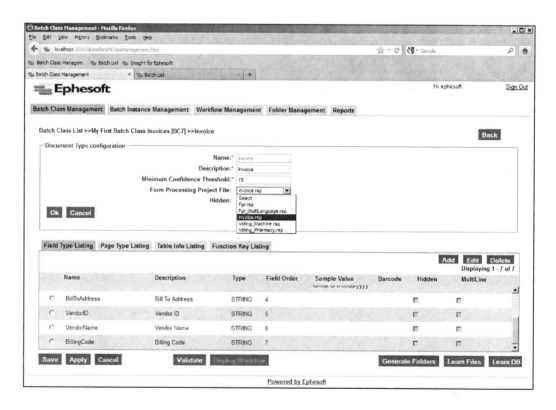

When you run a sample invoice through Ephesoft, you will see in validation that the value for the Billing Code is extracted.

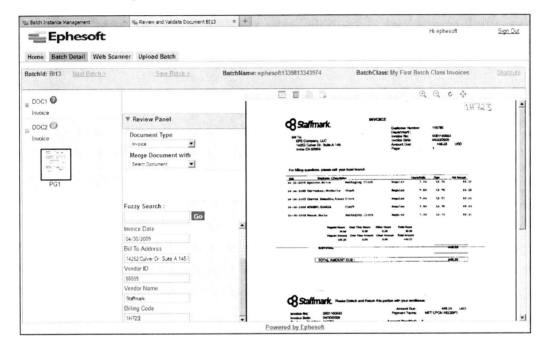

Table extraction

Table extraction is used to extract repeating information from a form. For example, we might want to extract the date, hours, rates, and total from each row of the following invoice.

 In order to perform table extraction, you must first turn on the Table Extraction switch in the `Table Extraction` plugin of the `Extraction` module.

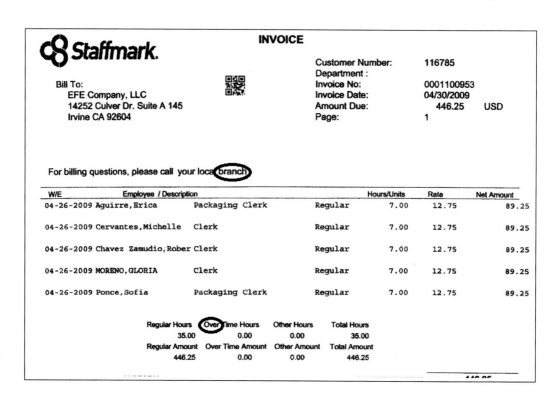

From the administrative interface, edit the batch class, edit the Invoice document type, and then select the **Table Info Listing** tab. Click on the **Add** button to define a new repeating set of fields to extract. Ephesoft will prompt for a name as well as a start pattern and an end pattern. The start pattern is a regular expression or word that is at the beginning of the table. The end pattern is a regular expression or a word that is consistently at the end of the table.

In the example above, the start pattern is the word "branch" and the word "Over" is the end pattern. We chose not to use the pattern "Regular" or "Hours" as the end pattern because both are used elsewhere on the page.

Ephesoft matches patterns in tables slightly differently than elsewhere in the system; you can match patterns with spaces in them for row patterns. If the end pattern is not found, Ephesoft will capture the table lines from all the pages of the document.

Extraction of rows can be enabled by a combination of a regular expression, column header, and column coordinates. In most cases you will use a combination of regular expressions with column headers.

Next create a new **Table Column Info** entry for each item to extract. In the **Table Columns Info Listing**, click on **Add** and enter the following information:

Date is simple, as it has a unique pattern; specify the pattern of \d{2}-\d{2}-\d{4}. It has a header pattern of W\/E.

The hours field has a pattern of \d.\d but there is more than one value for this pattern. In this case, we can specify a **Between Left** rule, meaning there is some string or pattern to the left of the value. In this case, the pattern is Regular. It has a header pattern of Hours\/Units.

The rate field has a pattern of \d{2}\.\d{2} and has a Between Left pattern of \d{1}\.\d{2} and a Between Right pattern of \d{2}\.\d{2}. It has a header pattern of Rate.

Finally, the total has a pattern of \d{2}\.\d{2} and a Between Left pattern of \d{2}\.\d{2}. It has a header pattern of Net Amount.

Once the rules are created, press the **Apply** button to save the configuration. To test the rule, place some sample documents in the batch class' `test table` folder, which is located here:

```
SharedFolders/%BatchClassIdentifer%/test-table
```

Go back to the **Table Info Listing** tab for this document type, select the table extraction rule to test and press the **Test Table** button. The results will pop up in a table as shown in the following screenshot:

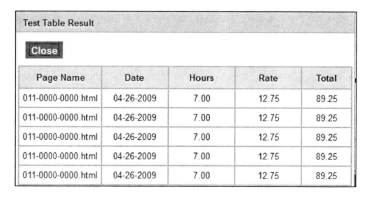

Page Name	Date	Hours	Rate	Total
011-0000-0000.html	04-26-2009	7.00	12.75	89.25
011-0000-0000.html	04-26-2009	7.00	12.75	89.25
011-0000-0000.html	04-26-2009	7.00	12.75	89.25
011-0000-0000.html	04-26-2009	7.00	12.75	89.25
011-0000-0000.html	04-26-2009	7.00	12.75	89.25

 Repeating fields extracted using table extraction cannot be sent to your CMS using the CMIS plugin; use scripting or an alternate export plugin.

It's easy to miss the indication for an extracted table in the operator's interface to Ephesoft. An icon is displayed next to the non-repeating extracted fields. Click on the icon to view the table data.

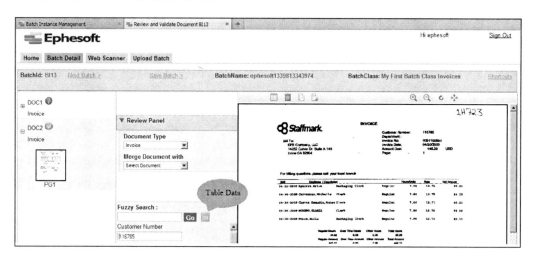

Ephesoft displays the extracted table content. Operators can edit cells, or edit and remove table rows to ensure that everything was captured properly.

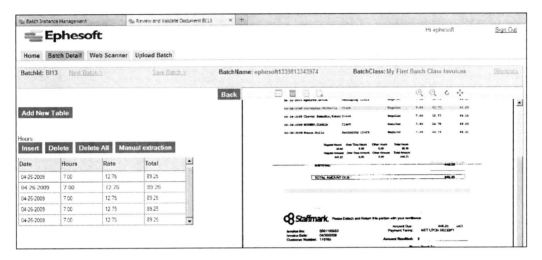

Scripting

Ephesoft can be configured to execute custom Java code in three places: in the workflow (at specific pre-defined points), when the fields change in validation, or when an operator presses a function key. This code can manipulate the documents, populate field values, integrate with external systems, normalize data, and so on.

Workflow scripts

The **MailroomAutomationTemplate** batch class, which we copied to create our custom batch, is configured with hooks to execute your own code in several places. For instance, if you want to perform a custom operation prior to export, you can edit the following file:

```
SharedFolders/%BatchClassIdentifer%/scripts/ScriptExport.java
```

This file contains the implementation of a class named `ScriptExport`. Whenever Ephesoft performs an export, it will call the `execute` method of this class.

```
public class ScriptExport implements IJDomScript {
  public Object execute(Document jdomObj,
                        String methodName,
                        String docIdentifier) {
    // execute custom code here
  }
}
```

You do not need to compile your Java code or restart Ephesoft in order for any changes to the script to take effect. Ephesoft will detect any changes to the file prior to execution and re-compile the code automatically.

The following scripts are available for customization:

- `ScriptAddNewTable.java`

- `ScriptAutomaticValidation.java`

- `ScriptDocumentAssembler.java`

- `ScriptExport.java`

- `ScriptExtraction.java`

- `ScriptFieldValueChange.java`

- `ScriptFunctionKey.java`

- `ScriptPageProcessing.java`

- `ScriptReview.java`

- `ScriptValidation.java`

> The default behavior in the ScriptAutomaticValidation script invalidates values based on types. Unfortunately, when you save the batch in the operator's validation screen, this script does not re-run. As a result, you can turn fields that had a red error indicator to green by just saving the document.
>
> We recommend that you study this script to learn how to manipulate the batch, and then disable all the functionality of the script. To best validate field values, you should create regular expressions in the **Regular Expression Listings** section of the administrative interface; this is part of editing a document type.

Ephesoft persists the state of each batch instance to the file system as an XML file. When Ephesoft executes a script, it passes a JDOM document object to the `execute` method. That document object is the result of parsing the XML file that represents the batch instance state. The author of a script can traverse this structure to determine metadata values, confidence levels, page counts, and so on. Scripts can also change the state of a batch instance by modifying the JDOM object and then overwriting Ephesoft's batch instance state file with the XML representation of that JDOM document object.

There is no documented schema for this XML structure. An Ephesoft batch XML file includes a `Document` element for each of the documents in the batch. A child element named `Identifier` specifies the ID of the document with which the `Document` element block is associated. Each `Document` element also includes a child `DocumentLevelField` element for each metadata field associated with the document. Various sub-elements of the `DocumentLevelField` element define the characteristics of the field.

For example, consider the table extraction performed in the previous section. Suppose you want to add up the hours from each row of the invoice and store the total in a metadata field named `TotalHours`. Here is what the batch instance state looks like when persisted to XML:

```
<Batch>
  <Documents>
    <Document>
      <Identifier>DOC1</Identifier>
      <DocumentLevelFields>
        <DocumentLevelField>
          <Name>TotalHours</Name>
          <Value>0.0<Value>
        </DocumentLevelField>
      </DocumentLevelFields>
      <DataTables>
        <DataTable>
          <Name>LaborTable</Name>
          <Rows>
            <Row>
              <Columns>
                <Column><Value>04-26-2009</Value></Column>
                <Column><Value>12.75</Value></Column>
                <Column><Value>7.00</Value></Column>
              </Columns>
            </Row>
            <!-- more rows here -->
          </Rows>
```

```
            </DataTable>
          </DataTables>
        </Document>
     </Documents>
   </Batch>
```

The actual XML file contains significantly more information; we have reduced the
content to just the elements that are relevant to this example. Here is an example of
some code that would sum up all the hours in the Hour cells and calculate that total
into the TotalHours field:

```java
public Object execute(Document jdomObj, String
                               methodName,
                    String docId)
{
  try {

    // for each invoice document
    String docPathStr =
      "/Batch/Documents/Document[Type='Invoice']";
    XPath docxPath = XPath.newInstance(docPathStr);
    for (Element doc :  docPath.selectNodes(jdomObj)) {

      // for each "hours" cell in the hours table
      String valuePathStr =
        "DataTables/DataTable[Name='Hours']" +
        "/Rows/Row/Columns/Column[2]/Value";
      XPath valuexPath = XPath.newInstance(valuePathStr);
      double totalHours = 0;
      for (Element hoursElement: valuexPath.selectNodes(doc)) {
       // add the hours to the total
       totalHours += Double.parseDouble(hoursElement.getText());
      }

      // write the total hours into a metadata field
      String ttlString =
        "DocumentLevelFields/" +
        "DocumentLevelField[Name='TotalHours']/Value";
      XPath ttlxPath = XPath.newInstance(ttlString);
      Element ttlElem = (Element) ttlXpath.selectSingleNode(doc);
      ttlElem.setText(String.valueOf(totalHours));
    }

    // persist the changed batch instance state
    writeToXML(document);

    // this is how we signal successful completion to Ephesoft
    return null;
  }
```

```
catch (JDOMException e) {
  System.err.println("script failed: " + e);
  e.printStackTrace();
  return e;
 }
}
```

This script first iterates across all the documents of type `Invoice`. Then it finds the `hours` cell for each row and adds that value to a running total. Next, it finds the `TotalHours` field and sets the field's value to be that total. Finally, it calls `writeToXML` to save this change to the batch instance. Ephesoft provides the `writeToXML` function; it is already in the `ScriptExport.java` file.

This script has also been simplified. In practice, you will discover that Ephesoft does not provide a `Value` tag for empty fields. Your script will need to call JDOM to add the `Value` tag to the `TotalHours` field before setting its value.

> Scripts used in validation such as `FunctionKey.java` or `Validation.java` can update the `errormessage` tag in the batch XML to display error messages to the user on the screen.

The result is that the `TotalHours` is populated if the values have been extracted from the table.

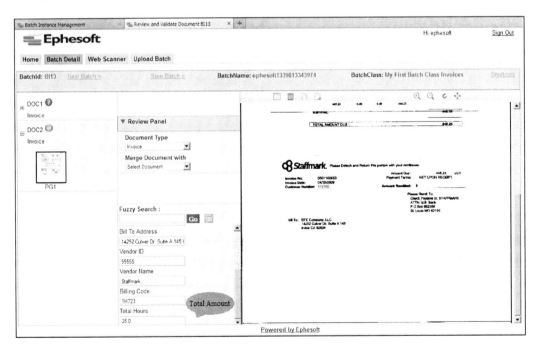

Triggering scripts when a field is edited

Ephesoft can call a script when a change is made to a value of a field in the validation screen.

 To use this feature, you must first turn on the Field Value Change Script switch in the `Validate Document` plugin of the `Validate Document` module.

Once that setting is saved, the `ScriptFieldValueChange.java` will be evoked when a field value changes in the validation screen. The following example will check to see if the field is of type "DATE" and if so, change any date formatted with "-" to "/". The script will run when the value is changed in the text field and the focus changes to another field, the document is saved (*Ctrl + Q* or *Ctrl + S*), or another document is selected.

For the following document, the value was modified by an operator to be in a date format with "-" as the separator.

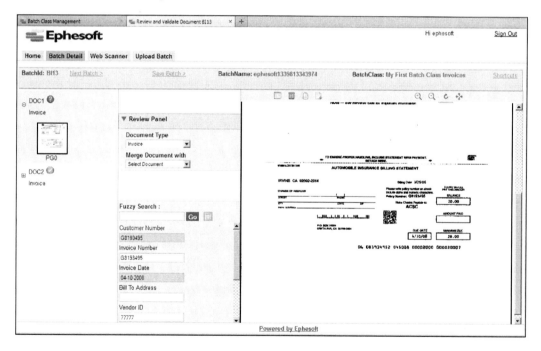

After the script runs, the format of the date changes to have "/" rather than "-".

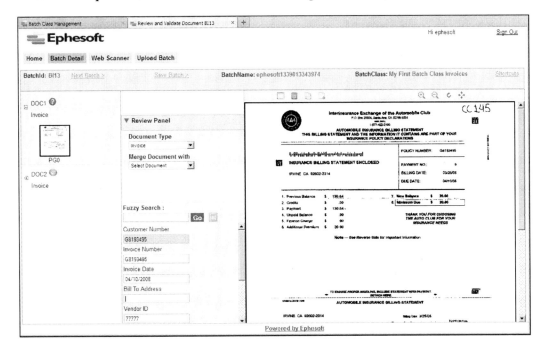

The following is the `ScriptFieldValueChange.java` used to format the date fields:

```
public void changeField(Document jdomObj, String fieldName,
                        String docId) {
  try {

    // find the field element that the operator is editing
    String fieldStr =
      "/Batch/Documents/Document[Identifier = '" + docId +
      "']/DocumentLevelFields/DocumentLevelField[Name = '" +
      fieldName + "']";
    XPath fieldxPath = XPath.newInstance(fieldStr);
    Element fieldElement =
      (Element) fieldxPath.selectSingleNode(jdomObj);

    // if this is a date
    XPath typexPath = XPath.newInstance("Type");
    Element typeNode =
      (Element) typexPath.selectSingleNode(fieldElement);
    String type = typeNode.getValue();
    if ("DATE".equals(type)) {
```

```
  // get the value
  XPath valuePath = XPath.newInstance("Value");
  Element valueNode =
    (Element)valuePath.selectSingleNode(fieldElement);
  String oldValue = valueNode.getValue();

  // reformat the date
  SimpleDateFormat oldFormat =
    new SimpleDateFormat("MM-dd-yyyy");
  SimpleDateFormat newFormat =
    new SimpleDateFormat("MM/dd/yyyy");
  Date date = oldFormat.parse(oldValue.trim());
  String newValue = newFormat.format(date);

  // persist the reformatted value
  valueNode.setText(newValue);
  writeToXML(jdomObj);
  }
}
catch (JDOMException x) {
 x.printStackTrace();
}
catch (ParseException x) {
  // format of date is not MM-dd-yyyy; ok to ignore
}
}
```

Triggering scripts from a function key

Ephesoft can call a script when a function key (*F1-F11*, excluding *F5*) is pressed. The function key mapping can be created for each document type. To create a function key mapping, first select a document and go to the **Edit** screen. When you configure this mapping, Ephesoft will also add a button to the validation area of the operator's interface that you can click on with a mouse to perform the same function.

- Select the **Function Key Listing** tab on the document type you would like to add a function key trigger.

- Click on the **Add** button. The **Plugin Details** page appears, as shown in the following screenshot:

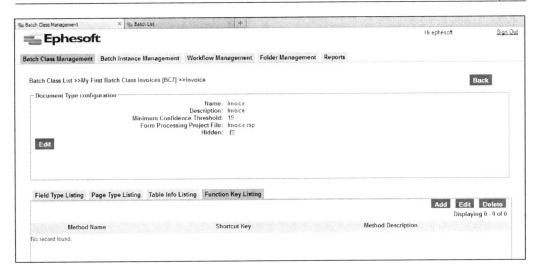

- Enter the **Method Name** (Java method in the `ScriptFunctionKey.java` file), **Shortcut Key** (*F1-F11*, excluding *F5*), and **Method Description**.
- Click on the **Ok** button. Then, click on the **Apply** button to save the configuration.

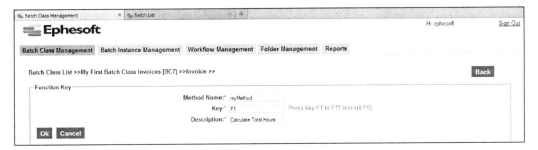

When the *F1* key is pressed in the review or validation screen, the following method will be executed. For a function key method, Ephesoft passes in the document identifier of the document selected by the operator and the DOM object of the batch XML document. This method uses the document identifier to locate the document that the operator has selected. Once the document is found, this method totals the hours in the labor table and saves the results in the `TotalHours` field (just as in the earlier example).

```java
public void myMethod(String docId, Document jdomObj) {
  try {

    // for each invoice document
    String docsPathStr =
      "/Batch/Documents/Document[Identifier='" + docId + "']";
```

```
XPath documentsPath = XPath.newInstance(docsPathStr);
for (Element doc : documentsPath.selectNodes(jdomObj)) {

  // for each "hours" cell in the labor table
  String valuePathStr =
    "DataTables/DataTable[Name='Hours']" +
    "/Rows/Row/Columns/Column[2]/Value";
  XPath valuexPath = XPath.newInstance(valuePathStr);
  double totalHours = 0;
  for (Element hoursElement: valuexPath.selectNodes(doc)) {

    // add the hours to the total
    totalHours += Double.parseDouble(hoursElement.getText());
  }

  // write the total hours into a metadata field
  String ttlPathStr =
    "DocumentLevelFields/" +
    "DocumentLevelField[Name='Hours']/Value";
  XPath ttlxPath = XPath.newInstance(ttlPathStr);
  Element ttlElement =
    (Element) ttlxPath.selectSingleNode(doc);

  // if there is no value element, create one
  if (ttlElement == null) {
   Element valueElement = new Element("Value");
   String fieldStr =
     "DocumentLevelFields/DocumentLevelField[Name='Hours']";
   XPath fieldxPath = XPath.newInstance(fieldStr);
   Element fieldElement =
     (Element) fieldxPath.selectSingleNode(doc);
   fieldElement.addContent(3, valueElement);
   ttlElement = valueElement;
  }

  ttlElement.setText(String.valueOf(totalHours));
 }

 // persist the changed batch instance state
 writeToXML(jdomObj);
}
catch (JDOMException e) {
 System.err.println("script failed: " + e);
 e.printStackTrace();
}
}
```

Now, looking at the operator's interface, you see an *F1* button. Press the table icon to view the table extraction value for the labor table.

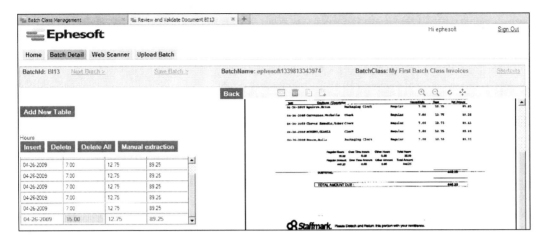

In the table results for the validation, you can add a new line by pressing the **Insert** button. Enter 15.0 in the Hours column and then press the **Back** button. The total displayed in the TotalHours field is incorrect, but if we press the *F1* key the TotalHours will be recalculated to include the new row in the labor table.

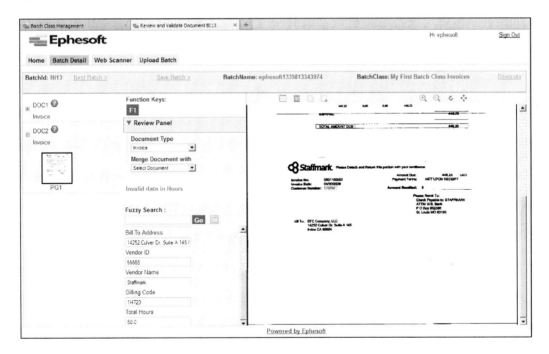

External application integration

There are many document classification scenarios in which certain types of documents cannot be properly indexed without metadata obtained from external data sources. It may be that the required document metadata cannot be extracted directly from the document content, or that extracted metadata may need to be validated by users with the help of data from an external system prior to the completion of an indexing activity. Regardless of the exact scenario, it is often helpful for the users of Ephesoft performing the indexing activity to be able to look up from external systems, using the Ephesoft validation screen.

For instance, mortgage companies are required to process various types of ad-hoc or trailing documents. Indexing users at these companies may require access to a customer database in order to properly associate a customer or loan ID with the document. In this scenario, it is essential for the indexing users to have search-level access to the customer information data source. Fortunately, Ephesoft provides the ability to access and integrate with external applications from the Ephesoft validation screen.

Up to four external application links may be made to appear within the review panel of the validation screen in the operator interface. Links are rendered as buttons whose names can be customized using techniques described later in this section.

The following screenshot depicts a scenario in which an external application link has been configured to display as the word "Find".

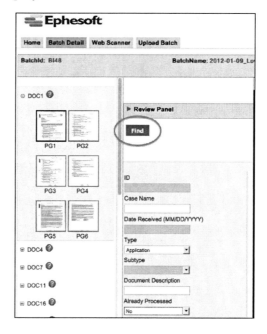

When an external application button is clicked, Ephesoft displays the external application within the validation screen as depicted in the following screenshot:

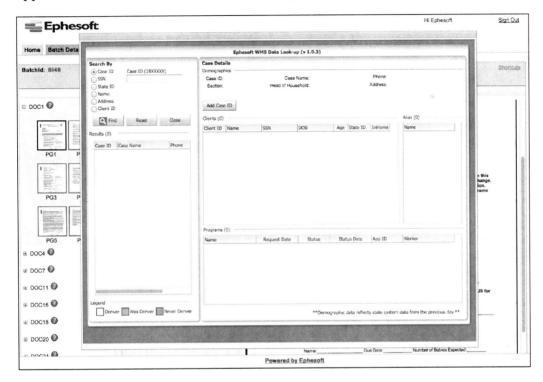

It is important to note that, because Ephesoft is itself a web-based application, it can only be configured to reference other web-based applications as external applications. External application links are configured separately for each batch class. The following sections describe how to perform this integration.

Configuring external application references

External applications are configured within the Ephesoft **Batch Class Management** screen. Edit the `Validate Document` plugin within the `Validate Document` module for your batch class.

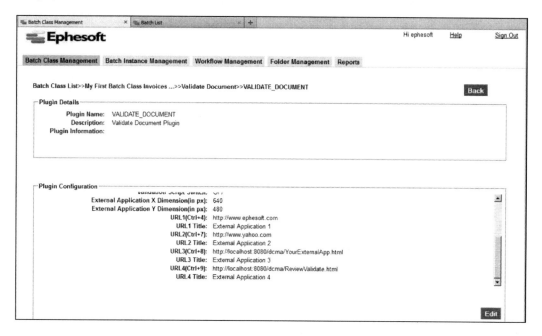

Click on the **Edit** button to modify the following properties:

- **External Application X Dimension**: This specifies the width in pixels of the dialog. All configured external applications are the same width.

- **External Application Y Dimension**: This specifies the height in pixels of the dialog. All configured external applications are the same height.

- **External Application Switch**: When a value of **OFF** is selected, no external application buttons will be displayed. When a value of **ON** is selected, then one button will be displayed for each URL field property field that includes a value.

- **URL1, URL2, URL3**, and **URL4**: These fields are used to specify the URLs for up to four external applications. A button will be presented in the batch verification form of a batch instance for each URL input field that is populated. The corresponding URL title fields are used to specify headers of the dialog boxes in which the external applications are displayed within Ephesoft. Titles are optional, so it is possible to leave these fields blank if no title is to be displayed for an external application dialog.

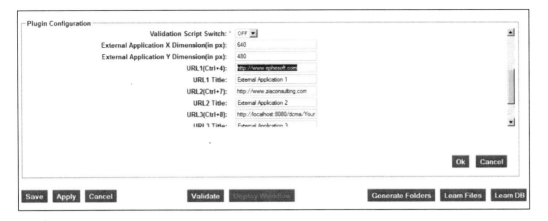

Once all of the desired configuration changes have been performed, click on the **OK** button within the **Plugin Configuration** panel and then click on the **Save** button.

 Like other batch class settings, the external application settings are applied only to new batch instances.

By default, the names of the external application buttons that are displayed within the batch validation screen are **App1**, **App2**, **App3**, and **App4**. These names are configurable on a deployment-wide basis within the C:\Ephesoft\Application\ i18n\rv\locale.js configuration file. Perform the following steps to update the button names:

1. Open the locale.js file with a text editor.

2. Locate the following constants:

   ° name_of_app_shortcut_ctrl_4 : "App1"

   ° name_of_app_shortcut_ctrl_7 : "App2"

   ° name_of_app_shortcut_ctrl_8 : "App3"

   ° name_of_app_shortcut_ctrl_9 : "App4"

3. Update the buttons' names as required.

4. Save and close the locale.js file.

5. Clear your browser cache.

6. Navigate to an applicable batch instance and verify that the new button names appear.

External application context

When a user clicks on one of the configured external application buttons within the batch validation screen, Ephesoft displays the body of the related external application within an embedded HTML *iframe* of the floating HTML div that makes up the visible boundary of the modal dialog. This is an important technical detail to take into consideration, because some web application frameworks will prevent an application from being displayed in an iframe unless explicit configuration changes are made to the framework configuration files. This source content protection mechanism is known as **frame busting**.

It is possible to pass static HTTP parameters to an external application. Simply include the required URL parameter name value pairs in the external application URLs that are configured within the plugin configuration interface described in the previous section. Ephesoft appends the following three URL parameters to any URL that you configure within an external application URL field:

- `document_id`: This parameter specifies Ephesoft's designation for the document that was being indexed at the time that the external application button was clicked (For example, DOC1). Please refer to the *Returning document metadata to Ephesoft* section in this chapter for more information on this parameter.

- `batch_xml_path`: This parameter specifies the absolute path to the batch XML metadata file on the Ephesoft server. Please refer to the *Returning document metadata to Ephesoft* section in this chapter for more information on this parameter.

- `ticket`: This parameter specifies a unique security token that the external application can use to verify that it is Ephesoft that is authorizing access to the external application. Please refer to the *Security tickets* section in this chapter for more information on this parameter.

The values of each of the parameters are URL encoded by Ephesoft. There is no impact to the Ephesoft application if these parameters aren't used by the external application.

Security tickets

Many external applications displayed by Ephesoft will present highly sensitive information to indexing users. It is, therefore, very likely that access to this type of external application is restricted within an enterprise. If restricted external applications are to allow their content to be revealed within the Ephesoft application, they need to ensure that the request is coming directly from the Ephesoft application.

The purpose of security tickets is to provide external applications with security tokens that:

- Can be validated by Ephesoft at the request of the external application
- Can be used only once
- Will expire after a period of time
- Are unique for every external application invocation

A unique security ticket is generated by Ephesoft each time a user clicks on the external application button and the unique value of the `ticket` URL parameter is passed to the external application. This ticket is only good for the period of one hour or until it is validated by Ephesoft at the request of the external application. The ticket is invalidated once used and it cannot be reused by browser debugging tools, or any other means that would represent unauthorized access to the external application.

The Ephesoft web application provides an authentication servlet that the external application can use to validate the tickets. The URL to invoke this servlet is:

```
http://<Ephesoft host>:<port>/dcma/authenticate?ticket=<ticket passed
to the external application>
```

> The `ticket` parameter value must be URL encoded twice before being submitted. Failure to encode the ticket value twice prior to submission to the authentication servlet will cause valid security tickets to be rejected.

The Ephesoft authentication servlet returns an HTTP response status code of 200, or **OK**, if the ticket is valid; and 401, or **Unauthorized**, if the ticket is not valid or has already been validated in a previous request.

> The URL that the external application should use in validating a ticket should be configured within the external application. The HTTP `referrer` header field value of an inbound HTTP request should never be trusted.
>
> The security tickets just provide a measure of certainty that the request is coming from a validated Ephesoft user. The external application needs to trust that Ephesoft has correctly restricted user access to each batch class and therefore to the buttons that call the external application.

Returning document metadata to Ephesoft

When Ephesoft invokes an external application URL, it appends the following two URL parameters to the end of the configured external application URL:

- `document_id`: This is the Ephesoft designation for the document that was being indexed in the batch at the instant that the external application button was clicked, for example, `DOC1`.

- `batch_xml_path`: This is the absolute path to the batch metadata XML file. This path is URL encoded. Here is an example of a batch XML path:
  `C:\Ephesoft\SharedFolders\ephesoft-system-folder\%BatchInstance Identifier%\%BatchInstanceIdentifier%_batch.xml`

External applications can make use of these parameters to manipulate Ephesoft's batch instance state using the same techniques we described in the *Scripting* section earlier in this chapter. The main difference is that external applications need to parse the XML file, whereas Ephesoft scripts receive a pre-parsed DOM representation of the XML.

External applications will need file system permission to access and modify the batch XML file.

In most cases, external applications will be hosted on a web application server that is hosted on a different server than the Ephesoft application. In these circumstances, it will be necessary to take into consideration the following three additional technical requirements for external application integration:

- The Ephesoft deployment must be configured to reference the system folder on a file system that is visible to the external application. This is often accomplished by putting the Ephesoft system folder on a network-accessible partition.

- The Ephesoft system folder must be made visible to the server that hosts the external application. To modify the batch state, the external application must have write privileges to the contents of system folder.

- Paths inside the batch XML file may need to be translated to be correct in the context of the external application. The path to the XML file may need the same translation.

For example, assume the external application wants to update the `LoanID` field of the document `DOC1` so the value is `XYZ123` instead of `AP38374-J2-221`. When the external application first opens the batch XML file, it might look as shown in the following code:

```
<Document>
  <Identifier>DOC1</Identifier>
    ...
  <DocumentLevelFields>
    <DocumentLevelField>
      <Name>LoanID</Name>
      <Type>STRING</Type>
      <Confidence>0.0</Confidence>
      <FieldOrderNumber>10</FieldOrderNumber>
      <FieldValueOptionList/>
      <Value>AP38374-J2-221</Value>
    </DocumentLevelField>
    ...
  </DocumentLevelFields>
    ...
</Document>
```

To update document-level indexing fields, the external application must first locate the `Document` element block in the batch XML file that is associated with the value of the `document_id` URL parameter that was passed to it by Ephesoft. Then the external application can examine each `Name` element of each `DocumentLevelField` element within the `Document` element block in order to locate the appropriate indexing field definitions. The value for a specific field is specified within the `DocumentLevelField` element block as a child element named `Value`. If no value has been specified, then the element won't exist and must be created by the external application. If a value has been specified, then the external application must replace the content of the `Value` element with the new value.

When the external application has completed making the necessary changes to the XML document model, it must write the updated document model to the batch XML file and close all related file streams. Failure to close streams may inhibit Ephesoft from performing further processing on the batch XML file.

Signalling dialog close and save events

Ephesoft displays all external applications in an HTML iframe. This iframe is embedded in a modal dialog preventing Ephesoft users from using the validation screen until the dialog is closed. Ephesoft provides no user interface controls that will enable application users to close the dialog. The external application must tell Ephesoft when the dialog should be closed.

The Ephesoft application provides a JavaScript function that can be called to close the dialog. This function is in the window HTML element, above the iframe in the DOM hierarchy. This function accepts a parameter whose value indicates how Ephesoft should interpret the event. The two accepted parameter values are:

- `Cancel`: This parameter closes the dialog with no refresh, for example, `window.top.postMessage("Cancel","*");`

- `Save`: This parameter closes the dialog with a document metadata refresh of the batch verification interface, for example, `window.top.postMessage("Save","*");`

Each external application user interface should at least include a **Cancel** or **Close** button that posts a cancel message to Ephesoft.

Custom workflow

Ephesoft comes with several batch classes, and each implements a workflow that is of general use. You can solve many business problems simply by copying one of the pre-configured batch classes and using the associated workflow. Sometimes, however, you need more steps (to accommodate specific needs of your organization) or fewer steps (to accelerate performance).

Adding a plugin to Ephesoft

Administrators can manage the plugins available in the system using the **Workflow Management** tab. Administrators can view all the available plugins and add new plugins to the system by uploading a ZIP file that contains all the files necessary to run a plugin for Ephesoft.

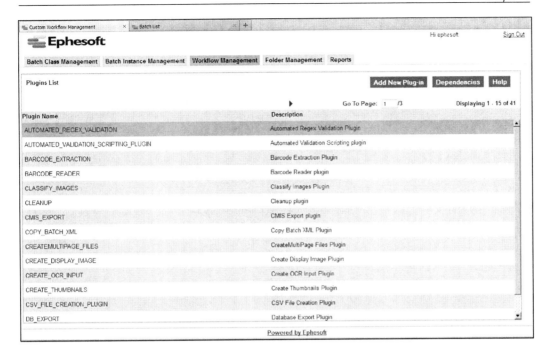

Click on the **Add New Plugin** button to upload ZIP files that contain a JAR file and an XML file containing the plugin details.

Plugins may be dependent on other plugins and these dependencies can be configured in the **Dependencies** window. Administrators can add, edit, or delete dependencies.

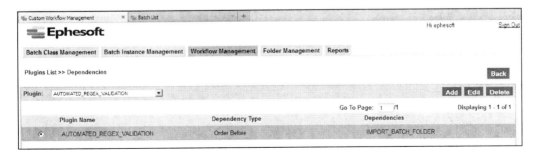

Customizing batch class workflows

Every batch class has its own capture workflow, which includes modules and plugins. Plugins are steps in the capture workflow and modules are used to group plugins to manage batches.

The following screenshot illustrates how administrators can add or remove modules to individual batch classes. Modules are simply groups of plugins; administrators can create modules by clicking on the **Add New Module** button.

Available Plugins: Whenever a plugin is selected in the available plugin list, that plugin and all of its dependencies will be highlighted. Clicking on the **Add** button will add the plugin and its dependencies to the selected list.

Selected Plugins: The selected plugins are displayed in the order of their execution. Administrators can use the **Up** and **Down** buttons to reorder the plugins or the **Remove** button to remove plugins from the module.

The administrator is required to validate and then deploy the new capture workflow. The **Validate** button will check all the dependencies for the selected plugins, and the **Deploy Workflow** button will deploy the workflow. Ephesoft will display dialogs confirming the operations completed successfully.

Writing a custom plugin

Ephesoft allows developers to write their own plugins and install them to Ephesoft. Developers should prepare the following files to install their custom plugins to Ephesoft:

- A JAR file containing code that will be executed in the workflow
- The Spring configuration to reference the code
- An XML file containing the plugin configuration, including: plugin name, jar name, dependencies, and version information

Plugins are packaged as ZIP files containing the above files so that administrators can upload and install the plugin to Ephesoft using workflow management.

The following is a sample plugin XML structure:

```xml
<?xml version="1.0" encoding="UTF-8"?>
<plugin>
  <jar-name>ephesoft-sample-plugin-0.0.1</jar-name>
  <plugin-name>EPHESOFT_SAMPLE_PLUGIN_TEST</plugin-name>
  <plugin-desc>Ephesoft Sample Plugin</plugin-desc>
  <plugin-workflow-name>EPHESOFT_SAMPLE_PLUGIN</plugin-workflow-name>
  <plugin-service-instance>samplePluginService</plugin-service-
instance>
  <method-name>sampleMethod</method-name>
  <is-scripting>false</is-scripting>
  <back-up-file-name>NA</back-up-file-name>
  <script-name>NA</script-name>
  <application-context-path>applicationContext-ephesoft-sample-plugin.
xml</application-context-path>
    <plugin-properties>
      <plugin-property>
        <name>samplePlugin.switch</name>
        <type>STRING</type>
        <description>Sample Plugin Switch</description>
        <is-mandatory>true</is-mandatory>
        <is-multivalue>false</is-multivalue>
        <!--1st sample value will be taken as default value -->
        <sample-values>
          <sample-value>OFF</sample-value>
        </sample-values>
        <sample-values>
          <sample-value>ON</sample-value>
        </sample-values>
      </plugin-property>
    </plugin-properties>
```

```
<dependencies>
  <dependency>
    <type-of-dependency>ORDER_BEFORE</type-of-dependency>
    <dependency-value>IMPORT_MULTIPAGE_FILES</dependency-value>
  </dependency>
</dependencies>
</plugin>
```

Take the following points into consideration when configuring your plugin:

- The `plugin-service-instance` should reference the bean ID of the Spring configuration to execute.

- The `application-context-path` should reference the Spring XML configuration file.

- All tags are required. The `is-scripting`, `is-mandatory`, and `is-multivalue` tags must have boolean values (TRUE or FALSE).

- The name of the file specified in the `jar-name` tag must match the JAR file present in the ZIP file.

- If the `is-scripting` tag has a value of TRUE, the values of the `back-up-file-name` and the `script-name` tag will be utilized.

- The `plugin-property` and `dependency` tags can have multiple instances.

Since Ephesoft plugins may use the results of other plugins, Ephesoft allows developers to specify dependencies in the XML file. Developers can create dependencies based on the plugin's position relative to another plugin in the workflow. Use the dependency type of `ORDER_BEFORE`, and set the value to the name of the plugin which this plugin should precede. If there should only be one instance of this plugin for each batch class use the dependency type of `UNIQUE` and set the value to TRUE.

To create the JAR file, developers are encouraged to use maven projects. The following steps are designed to create a sample plugin that outputs the "Hello World" example:

1. Create a Maven project with your favorite IDE such as Eclipse.

2. Enter the Artifact information as follows:

    a. Group Id: `com.ephesoft.dcma`

    b. Artifact Id: `ephesoft-sample-plugin`

    c. Version: `1.0.0`

    d. Packaging: `jar`

3. Once the project structure is created, create a new folder path `resources/`
`META-INF` under the `main` folder.

4. In the `META-INF` folder create a new file called `applicationContext-`
`ephesoft-sample-plugin.xml` with the following configuration:

```xml
<?xml version="1.0" encoding="UTF-8"?>
<beans default-autowire="byName" xsi:schemaLocation="http://
www.springframework.org/schema/beans http://www.springframework.
org/schema/beans/spring-beans-3.0.xsd http://www.springframework.
org/schema/util http://www.springframework.org/schema/util/
spring-util-3.0.xsd http://www.springframework.org/schema/
context http://www.springframework.org/schema/context/spring-
context-3.0.xsd http://www.springframework.org/schema/aop http://
www.springframework.org/schema/aop/spring-aop-3.0.xsd http://
www.springframework.org/schema/tx http://www.springframework.
org/schema/tx/spring-tx-3.0.xsd " xmlns:context="http://www.
springframework.org/schema/context" xmlns:aop="http://www.
springframework.org/schema/aop" xmlns:xsi="http://www.w3.org/2001/
XMLSchema-instance" xmlns:util="http://www.springframework.org/
schema/util" xmlns:p="http://www.springframework.org/schema/p"
xmlns:tx="http://www.springframework.org/schema/tx" xmlns="http://
www.springframework.org/schema/beans">

    <import resource="classpath:/META-INF/ephesoft-sample-plugin/
applicationContext.xml"/>
    </beans>
```

5. Under the `META-INF` folder create a folder named `ephesoft-sample-plugin`.

6. In the `ephesoft-sample-plugin` folder create a new file called
`applicationContext.xml` with the following configuration:

```xml
<?xml version="1.0" encoding="UTF-8"?>
<beans default-autowire="byName" xsi:schemaLocation="http://www.
springframework.org/schema/beans http://www.springframework.org/
schema/beans/spring-beans-3.0.xsd http://www.springframework.
org/schema/util http://www.springframework.org/schema/util/
spring-util-3.0.xsd http://www.springframework.org/schema/
context http://www.springframework.org/schema/context/spring-
context-3.0.xsd http://www.springframework.org/schema/aop http://
www.springframework.org/schema/aop/spring-aop-3.0.xsd http://
www.springframework.org/schema/tx http://www.springframework.
org/schema/tx/spring-tx-3.0.xsd " xmlns:context="http://www.
springframework.org/schema/context" xmlns:aop="http://www.
springframework.org/schema/aop" xmlns:xsi="http://www.w3.org/2001/
XMLSchema-instance" xmlns:util="http://www.springframework.org/
schema/util" xmlns:p="http://www.springframework.org/schema/p"
xmlns:tx="http://www.springframework.org/schema/tx" xmlns="http://
www.springframework.org/schema/beans">
```

```
<bean class="com.ephesoft.dcma.ephesoftSamplePlugin.service.
SamplePluginServiceImpl" id="samplePluginService">
</bean>

<context:component-scan base-package="com.ephesoft.dcma.
ephesoftSamplePlugin"/>
</beans>
```

7. Create a new package in the `main` folder as follows:

   - Source Folder: `ephesoft-sample-plugin/src/main/java`
   - Name: `com.ephesoft.dcma.ephesoftSamplePlugin.service`

8. Create a new class file named `SamplePluginService.java` in the package referenced above with the source code as follows:

```
package com.ephesoft.dcma.ephesoftSamplePlugin.service;
import com.ephesoft.dcma.da.id.BatchInstanceID;
public interface SamplePluginService {
  void sampleMethod(BatchInstanceID batchInstanceID,
      final String pluginWorkflow) throws Exception;
}
```

9. Create a new class file named `SamplePluginServiceImpl.java` in the package referenced above with the source code as follows:

```
package com.ephesoft.dcma.ephesoftSamplePlugin.service;
import com.ephesoft.dcma.da.id.BatchInstanceID;
public class SamplePluginServiceImpl implements
SamplePluginService {
  public void sampleMethod(BatchInstanceID batchInstanceID,
      String pluginWorkflow) throws Exception {
    System.out.println("*********Hello World*********");
  }
}
```

10. Create the JAR file by building the Maven build and make sure to include `Ephesoft.jar` in the Maven repository, and dependency for the Ephesoft in the `pom.xml`.

Grid computing

Ephesoft allows companies to implement a distributed capture system. Using distributed capture, documents can be imported or scanned at one location using local Ephesoft server(s) and the batch can be transferred to other Ephesoft servers for any subsequent workflow steps, such as page processing or export. Ephesoft is flexible enough that each module can be executed on a different set of Ephesoft servers.

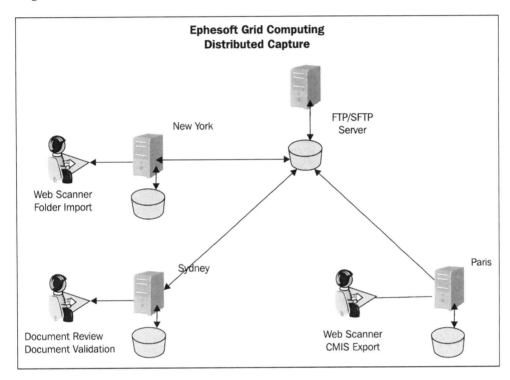

In the example above, documents are scanned in New York or Paris. Ephesoft uploads the batches (images) to a centrally-accessible FTP server. The server in Sydney downloads the documents for review and validation. Batches are then transferred to Paris for export.

To configure grid computing there are two relevant Ephesoft settings:

- On each server, edit the following file to reference the centrally-accessible FTP server: `C:\Ephesoft\Application\WEB-INF\classes\META-INF\dcma-ftp\dcma-ftp.properties`.

For each module that has a remote server, you will need to modify the module property values for the remote URL and the remote batch class identifier. The remote URL should be `http://%hostname%:%port%/dcma`, where hostname specifies the remote server and port specifies the port on which Ephesoft is configured to listen. The remote batch class identifier indicates which batch class on the remote server should continue processing the batch.

In the following example, we are configuring the New York Ephesoft server. The `Page Process` module's properties are changed to have the remote URL of the Sydney Ephesoft instance, which has the batch class identifier of `BC10`. On completion of the folder import module from New York, the batch will be transferred to the Sydney server for page processing.

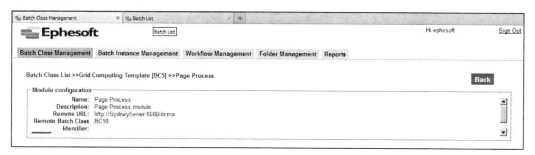

If a batch moves from one server to another and then the batch is restarted at a previous module in the workflow it will be executed on the server on which it currently resides.

Automatic learning

Automatic learning allows Ephesoft to create key/value extraction rules based on operator feedback in validation. This functionality can be enabled in the `Key Value Learning` plugin. As covered in previous chapters, key/value extraction rules require the following information:

- A regular expression for a key, an anchor point to find the desired value
- A regular expression for the value
- The location of the value relative to the location of the key

When the `Key Value Learning` plugin is enabled, Ephesoft will attempt to create extraction rules when an operator populates index metadata. Each time an Ephesoft operator uses the mouse to populate a field, Ephesoft searches the `dcma-value-regex.properties` file to find a regular expression that matches the selected value.

If a matching value is found, it will look at the `key_value.location_order` property of the `dcma-key-value-location.properties` file. The property will contain a value such as "TOP;LEFT" which will specify the order in which Ephesoft will search for the key. Ephesoft will look in the document being processed for text above (TOP) the selected value that matches a regular expression in the `dcma-key-regex.properties` file. If no matching text is found, Ephesoft will look to the left (LEFT) of the selected value. If Ephesoft is able to find a matching key value expression, it will create a key/value extraction rule.

The following example shows how the `Key Value Learning` plugin creates a key/value extraction rule based on user input in validation:

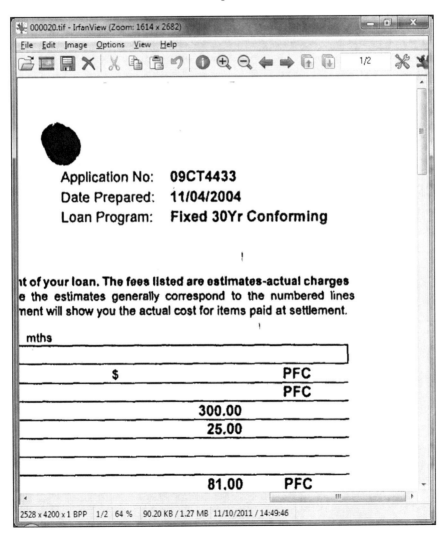

Suppose your system is configured as follows:

- `dcma-value-regex.properties: [0-9]{5,15}`

  `(0[1-9]|1[012])[- /.](0[1-9]|[12][0-9]|3[01])[- /.]\d\d([0-9]{2})?`

- `dcma-key-value-location.properties:`
  `key_value.location_order=TOP;LEFT;RIGHT`

- `dcma-key-regex.properties:`
  `Invoice`
  `Prepared`

Suppose, while populating the **Date Prepared** field in the validation screen, the operator selects the value **11/04/2004**. Ephesoft will match this text to the second regular expression in the `dcma-value-regex.properties` file. Ephesoft will then look above (TOP) this value for text that matches values in the `dcma-key-regex.properties` file. Since it does not find a match in that location, it will look to the left (LEFT) where it will find the text "Prepared" matching the second regular expression in `dcma-key-regex.properties`. Ephesoft will then create a key/value extraction rule with the following configuration:

- Key: `Prepared`

- Location: `RIGHT`

- Value: `(0[1-9]|1[012])[- /.](0[1-9]|[12][0-9]|3[01])[- /.]\d\d([0-9]{2})?`

 The location set in the extraction rule is the opposite of the value used to locate the key.

Summary

Congratulations! You can conquer almost any document capture task with the tools and skills now at your disposal. You should be able to configure Ephesoft to implement the scanning needs of most organizations, and you know how to customize and extend Ephesoft to handle anything that it cannot do *out of the box*.

In the next chapter, we will share some helpful tips including troubleshooting, administration, Active Directory / LDAP setup, and e-mail processing configuration.

7
Tips

Now that you have a thorough understanding of the Ephesoft system, it is time to turn our attention to some items that will prove helpful during the implementation and support of your system. In this chapter, we will provide helpful tips including the following:

- Troubleshooting
- Restarting a batch
- No blank forms for training
- Setting up Active Directory
- Setting up e-mail processing

Troubleshooting

In this section we explain common troubleshooting methods for Ephesoft.

Logging

The primary log file for Ephesoft is located here:

```
C:\Ephesoft\Application\dcma-all.log
```

Sometimes additional information can be found in these files:

- `C:\Ephesoft\JavaAppServer\logs\catalina.*.log`
- `C:\Ephesoft\JavaAppServer\logs\stdout_*.log`
- `C:\Ephesoft\JavaAppServer\logs\stderr_.*.log`

Ephesoft can be configured to log greater details by editing this file:

```
C:\Ephesoft\application\log4j.xml
```

Change the level from WARN to INFO, or for the most information, DEBUG.

```
<logger name=com.ephesoft>
  <level value=DEBUG />
</logger>
```

Monitoring batch progress

The **Batch Instance Management** tab of the administration interface shows the status of the batch, but without much detail. The status is not updated automatically; the list has to be refreshed manually.

Batch processing can also be monitored by configuring logging to the INFO level and watching the logs. If Cygwin is installed, you can *tail* the file. A light weight solution for those who are not comfortable with Unix is a Windows implementation of the tail program, such as BareTail. These can be found online at:

- `http://www.baremetalsoft.com/baretail/`
- `http://www.cygwin.com/`

A third way of monitoring batch progress is to look in the batch instance folder. First, find the batch's batch instance ID in the **Batch Instance Management** tab. This will begin with BI and end with a hexadecimal number. Then watch Ephesoft's working folder for that batch. If the batch ID is **BI99,** Ephesoft will write working files to this folder:

```
C:\Ephesoft\SharedFolders\ephesoft-system-folder\BI99
```

Sort the display to show the most recently modified files first; this will provide a good sense of what Ephesoft is doing.

Examining the batch file

The workflows persist workflow data (assembly information, extracted index field values, and so on) in an XML file for each batch. Each plugin creates a snapshot of this data when it executes. Look at the XML data to help debug assembly and extraction by looking at values, confidence level, and alternative values.

The batch files are stored in the batch instance working directory.

Restarting the batch

Failed batch instances can be restarted from an earlier step in the workflow using the administrative **Batch Instance Management** interface. This is faster than having to create a new batch instance.

For example, if a modification is made to a script in the workflow, restarting means a new workflow does not need to be started to test those changes.

No blank forms for training

Classification is most accurate when the system is trained with blank forms. If blank forms are not available, accurate classification can still be achieved.

Pressing **Learn Files** in the **Batch Class Management** administrative interface will cause Ephesoft to OCR the sample documents into a **HOCR** file. This is an HTML representation of the OCR output.

The HTML file can be edited to remove any content that is not part of the blank form. After the HTML file is updated, click on **Learn Files** again to update the index files used by Ephesoft. This will not overwrite the changes that have been made to the HTML file; that will only happen if the source TIFF is updated.

Setting up Active Directory

Ephesoft has the ability to integrate with Active Directory. In the following section, we will walk you through on how to set up this integration.

Directory server overview

The primary function of a directory server application is the storing of information about users and groups within an enterprise. This includes information about who these users are, what organizations they belong to, what groups they belong to, and what their login credentials are for a related domain. The idea is that rather than maintaining user information and credentials across many different systems and software applications, an IT enterprise includes a single directory server in order to centralize this information. Application systems defer to this server in order to authenticate users and obtain information about their group membership so that authorization may be granted within each context.

Information is organized in a hierarchical fashion within a directory. At the root level of the directory structure is a **domain component**, or **DC**, which is similar in concept to a disk volume name. The DC name conforms to the domain name that is applied to the server host domain. In accordance with LDAP conventions, the "." character is replaced by a comma and DC= is added as a prefix to each part of the name. Therefore, "ziaconsulting.com" becomes "DC=ziaconsulting,DC=com".

Folders within the directory structure are called **organizational units**, or **OUs**. They are containers for other OUs or user and group objects. Like folders, they are simply used in order to organize user and group objects so that they can be easily found and uniquely distinguished. Instead of using slashes as path separators, commas are used, and OU= is prefixed to each OU in the path. Another important thing to note is that directory paths are constructed from most specific to least specific order, which is the reverse of how one typically constructs file system folder paths. For example, the directory path "OU=SERVICE_ACCOUNTS,OU=DOMAIN_USERS,DC=ziaconsulting,DC=com" is visually represented as follows:

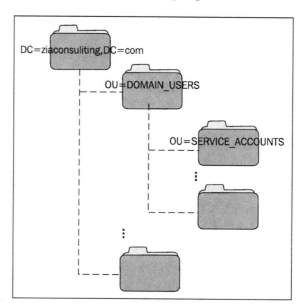

User and group objects within the directory structure have attributes associated with them that describe their characteristics. User attributes capture information such as the user's login ID, first name, last name, reporting manager, location, and so on. New attributes can be created on the fly in order to capture any information that should be shared with the applications that require that information. There are several core attributes that are defined for user objects:

- **CN** (*Common Name*): This attribute is typically used to capture a user's first name. It can be used for many other purposes, but it is used for first names within the enterprise.

- **SN** (*Surname*): This attribute is typically used to capture a user's last name.

- **UID** or **sAMAccountName** (*User login ID*): Either one of these attributes may be used to capture a users login ID within the domain. sAMAccountName is typically used within Microsoft Active Directory implementations of a directory server.

- **DN** (*Distinguished Name*): The DN is the unique name for the user within the directory. It represents the user object's unique path within the directory structure.

For example, `CN=ephesoft,OU=SERVICE_ACCOUNTS,OU=DOMAIN_` `USERS,DC=ziaconsulting,DC=com` uniquely identifies the "ephesoft" user object within the directory for the "`DC= ziaconsulting,DC=com`" domain.

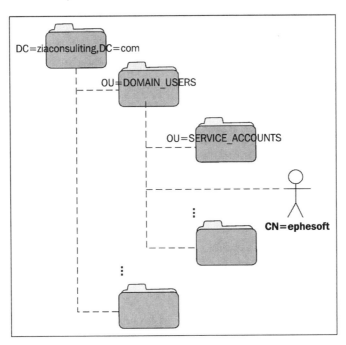

Group objects share many of the same attributes, though some attributes such as SN do not apply. The member attribute is unique to the group object. It may be repeated within a single group object as a way of persisting the DNs of all user objects who are members of the group.

LDAP

LDAP, or **Lightweight Directory Access Protocol,** is a standards-based protocol for communicating with a directory server. The structure of the protocol itself is not important, because the details of that protocol are hidden behind an API in all practical applications of the protocol. However, you should understand that it can be used to authenticate users, search directory paths, and view object attributes. Directory servers monitor configured TCP ports on host servers for inbound LDAP requests. SSL may be employed within the transport layer in order to ensure encrypted communication between the server and the client. An SSL-enabled LDAP connection is referred to as an LDAPS connection.

Ephesoft LDAP connector configuration

Ephesoft is delivered with an embedded OpenLDAP directory server. In fact, the LDAP connector of the application is always in use by the Ephesoft application even when it is not configured to point to an external directory server. Therefore, configuring Ephesoft to reference an external directory server for user authentication and group membership is a matter of modifying existing Ephesoft configuration files. The Ephesoft installation process pre-configures this to reference and integrate with the internal directory server.

Ephesoft directory server service account

In order to be able to authenticate users and/or determine if users are members of directory server groups, it is necessary for Ephesoft to connect to the LDAP using a service account. This service account is identified by a DN and a password. Therefore, be sure to obtain the DN and password for this service account prior to an Ephesoft LDAP configuration attempt. The service account in the previous example is:

```
CN=ephesoft,OU=SERVICE_ACCOUNTS,OU=DOMAIN_
USERS,DC=ziaconsulting,DC=com
```

Ephesoft directory server groups

Ephesoft must be configured to locate groups within the directory so that it might examine the `member` attribute values for each group and determine if an authenticated user is a member of those groups. Group membership is required in order for users to gain access to batches that are ready for verification in any one of the configured batch classes, or to perform administrative activities within the administrative interfaces of the application.

It is a requirement of the Ephesoft LDAP implementation that the DNs associated with directory user objects that are to be considered members of the group be added directly as new `member` attribute values to a related group. It is not sufficient to add the DN of another group as a member attribute of the Ephesoft group in order for users who are members of that group to be considered members of the Ephesoft group. The concept of nested groups is not recognized within the Ephesoft LDAP implementation.

Ephesoft LDAP configuration files

There are three configuration files associated with the Ephesoft LDAP configuration that must be updated in order for Ephesoft to reference an external directory server. Once these files are updated, none of the user accounts defined in the embedded OpenLDAP directory server may be used to login to Ephesoft (the Ephesoft user being the most notable).

- `C:\Ephesoft\JavaAppServer\conf\Catalina\localhost\dcma.xml`

This configuration file not only defines the Ephesoft application context within the embedded Tomcat application server, but also defines the LDAP security realm for the application. Ephesoft leverages Tomcat's built-in security realm capability in order to authenticate users and obtain information about their directory server group memberships.

- `C:\Ephesoft\Application\WEB-INF\classes\META-INF\dcma-user-connectivity\user-connectivity.xml`

This file defines the LDAP configuration for the Ephesoft LDAP connector so that it is able to find Ephesoft related groups in the LDAP. The list of groups found in LDAP using these settings is used to populate the "roles" list within the Ephesoft **Batch Class Management** interface. The roles selected in this list define the groups of users who have access to the related batch class.

- `C:\Ephesoft\Application\WEB-INF\web.xml`

This configuration file not only defines the Java web application context for the entire Ephesoft application, but it also defines role-based security constraints on specific Ephesoft interfaces.

The following sections define how these configuration files are edited in order to communicate with a Microsoft Active Directory server.

dcma.xml

The following XML illustrates sample settings for the dcma.xml configuration file:

```
<Context path="/dcma" docBase="E:\Ephesoft\Application"
debug="10" privileged="false">
    <Realm className="org.apache.catalina.realm.JNDIRealm"
debug="99"
        connectionURL="ldap://elm.ziaconsulting.com:3268"
    connectionName="CN=ephesoft,OU=SERVICE_ACCOUNTS,OU=DOMAIN_
USERS,DC=ziaconsulting,DC=com"
        connectionPassword="secret"
        referrals="follow"
        userBase="OU=DOMAIN_USERS,DC=ziaconsulting,DC=com "
        userSearch="(sAMAccountName={0})"
        userSubtree="true"
    roleBase="OU=APPLICATION_SPECIFIC,OU=SECURITY,OU=DOMAIN_
GROUPS,DC=ziaconsulting,DC=com"
        roleName="cn"
        roleSearch="(member={0})"
        roleSubtree="true"/>
</Context>
```

Only the attributes of the Realm element are to be modified in this file. Always create a backup to the file prior to making modifications. If the backup file is retained in the C:\Ephesoft\JavaAppServer\conf\Catalina\localhost folder along with the original, then be sure to change the file extension to something other than .xml.

The following table defines the purpose of each configuration attribute of the Realm element:

Attribute	Description
connectionURL	Specifies the protocol and URL for connecting to the Microsoft Active Directory server. **ldap** indicates that the protocol is LDAP. If LDAP over SSL is employed, then change the protocol designation from ldap to ldaps. The related SSL certificate must be installed in the Java trusted keyStore in order for the ldaps protocol to be used.
connectionName	Specifies the DN of the user object in the directory that is associated with the service account used by Ephesoft to connect to the directory server.

Attribute	Description
connectionPassword	Specifies the password for the user object in the directory that is associated with the service account used by Ephesoft to connect to the directory server.
referrals	Specifies whether the driver should search from the domain root of Active Directory for users. This attribute must be set to a value of follows when the target directory server is a Microsoft Active Directory (as in this example).
userBase	Specifies the DN of the base directory where the user search should begin. We would like Ephesoft to authenticate all domain users, so the value of this attribute is set to "OU=DOMAIN_USERS,DC=ziaconsulting,DC=com". Only user accounts that reside in this OU or a sub-OU will be visible.
userSearch	Specifies the attribute filter that should be used to find the user object within the directory. The {0} text is substituted with the user-entered login ID during the authentication process. Therefore, the fundamental purpose of this configuration value is to identify the attribute name of the user object in the Microsoft Active Directory server that should be matched to the user-entered text for the login ID.
userSubtree	Indicates that the search for the user object should include any sub-directory structure that may exist below the specified userBase DN.
roleBase	Specifies the base DN in the directory server where the Ephesoft roles can be found.
roleName	Specifies the group object attribute that defines the group name. Within the Microsoft Active Directory server, it is typical for both the sAMAccountName and cn attributes to be used for the group name.
roleSearch	Specifies the attribute filter that should be used within a group object context in order to determine if a user is a member of the group. The member attribute of a group object is typically used within Microsoft Active Directory server for this purpose. It is this attribute value that is set to the DN of a user object in order to indicate group membership, so we set this filter value to member={0}. {0} is substituted with the user object DN.
roleSubtree	Indicates that group objects within sub-directories of the configured "roleBase" should be examined for user membership.

Once this configuration file has been updated, it is necessary to restart the Tomcat server that hosts the Ephesoft application in order for the changes to take effect. If the configuration is incorrect, then it will not be possible to login to Ephesoft using valid Active Directory credentials.

user-connectivity.xml

The following text illustrates sample settings for the user-connectivity.xml configuration file:

```
user.ldap_url=ldap://localhost:389
user.ldap_config=com.sun.jndi.ldap.LdapCtxFactory
user.ldap_domain_component_name=ephesoft
user.ldap_domain_component_organization=com
user.msactivedirectory_url=ldap://elm.ziaconsulting.com:3268
user.msactivedirectory_config=com.sun.jndi.ldap.LdapCtxFactory
user.msactivedirectory_context_path=OU=APPLICATION_
SPECIFIC,OU=SECURITY,OU=DOMAIN_GROUPS
user.msactivedirectory_domain_component_name=ziaconsulting
user.msactivedirectory_domain_component_organization=com
user.msactivedirectory_user_name=CN=ephesoft,OU=SERVICE_
ACCOUNTS,OU=DOMAIN_USERS,DC=ziaconsulting,DC=com
user.msactivedirectory_password=secret
# filter can have |(OR), &(AND) and !(NOT)
# |  (|(cn=a*))
# &  (&(cn=a*))
# !  (!(cn=a*))
# complex example ((!(cn=a*))(|(cn=ephesoft*)(&(cn=b*)))
user.msactivedirectory_group_search_filter=((cn=Ephesoft*))
user.tomcatUserXmlPath=C:\\Ephesoft\\JavaAppServer\\conf\\tomcat-
users.xml
# 0 for LDAP
# 1 for MS Active Directory
# 2 for Tomcat
user.connection=1
```

The properties that begin with user.ldap and user.tomcat may be ignored in this configuration file, as they pertain to the default settings for the embedded OpenLDAP directory server. Always back up the user-connectivity.xml file before making changes to the file. If the backup file is retained in the C:\Ephesoft\ Application\WEB-INF\classes\META-INF\dcma-user-connectivity\user-connectivity.xml folder along with the original, then be sure to change the file extension to something other than .xml.

The following table defines the purpose of each pertinent configuration property:

Attribute	Description
user.msactivedirectory_url	Specifies the protocol and URL for connecting to the Microsoft Active Directory server. ldap indicates that the protocol is LDAP. If LDAP over SSL is employed, then change the protocol designation from ldap to ldaps. The related SSL certificate must be installed in the Java trusted keyStore in order for the ldaps protocol to be used.
user.msactivedirectory_ config	Specifies the name of the LDAP context implementation class to use. In this case, the built-in Oracle Java class is being referenced.
user.msactivedirectory_ context_path	Specifies the base DN, minus the DC designations, in the directory server where the Ephesoft roles may be found. Multiple paths may be specified. Use ";;" as a delimiter between each of the specified paths.
user.msactivedirectory_ domain_component_name	Specifies the DC below the root DC, or ziaconsulting in our case since the full domain is DC=ziaconsulting,DC=com.
user.msactivedirectory_ domain_component_ organization	Specifies the root DC, or com in our case since the full domain is DC=ziaconsulting,DC=com.
user.msactivedirectory_user_ name	Specifies the DN of the directory server account that should be used for querying the directory. In this example, the Microsoft Active Directory service account user is "ephesoft" which has a DN of CN=ephesoft,OU=SERVICE_ ACCOUNTS,OU=DOMAIN_ USERS,DC=ziaconsulting,DC=com.
user.msactivedirectory_ password	Specifies the password associated with the service account specified in the previous property.

Attribute	Description
user.msactivedirectory_ group_search_filter	Specifies a filter that may be used to filter the names of groups that may appear in the Ephesoft directory server group list – the "roles" list in the **Batch Class Management** interface. In this example, all of the Ephesoft group names begin with "Ephesoft", and the cn attribute of the group object specifies the group name in the Microsoft Active Directory. Therefore, the filter ((cn=Ephesoft*)) may be specified to ensure that only group names that start with "Ephesoft" are included in the list.
user.connection	Specifies which type of source Ephesoft should use for obtaining the list of groups. A value of 1 is specified as the value of this property, so that the user.msactivedirectory properties are utilized.

Once this configuration file has been updated, it is necessary to restart the Tomcat server that hosts the Ephesoft application in order for the changes to take effect.

To verify that the configuration is correct:

1. Navigate to the **Batch Class Management** interface for the deployment: `http://%hostname%:%port%/dcma/BatchClassManagement.html`
2. Login using valid directory server credentials.
3. Select one of the batch classes and click on the **Edit** button.
4. Click on the **Edit** button that appears in the **Batch Class Configuration** panel.
5. The Role listbox will display each of the Ephesoft groups.

Highlight one or more roles in this list to ensure that users associated with this directory server groups have access to the related batch class.

web.xml

This configuration file not only defines the Java web application context for the entire Ephesoft application, but also defines role-based security constraints on specific Ephesoft interfaces. Each security constraint is defined in a `security_constraint` configuration block similar to the following:

```
<security-constraint>
  <web-resource-collection>
    <web-resource-name>batch class management</web-resource-name>
    <url-pattern>/BatchClassManagement.html</url-pattern>
```

```
      <http-method>GET</http-method>
      <http-method>POST</http-method>
   </web-resource-collection>
   <auth-constraint>
      <role-name>Ephesoft_Admin</role-name>
   </auth-constraint>
</security-constraint>
```

It is the `role-name` element which specifies the directory server group to which the related interface is restricted. Therefore, in the previous example, the **Batch Class Management** interface is restricted to members of the **Ephesoft_Admin** group. This same role name must be specified for the following security constraint web resources (identified by the `web-resource-name` element):

- batch class management
- batch instance management
- web scanner
- reporting
- upload batch

After making updates to the `web.xml` file, you must restart the Tomcat service in order for those changes to take effect.

Troubleshooting

If you find that you are having problems verifying the LDAP connector settings in either of these files, then download and install a free directory server management application such as Apache Directory Studio, and use the application to debug your settings. Directory Studio includes a search capability which functions using filters similar to those that were populated in the XML files.

Setting up e-mail processing

Ephesoft has the ability to poll POP3 and IMAP accounts. If Ephesoft finds new mail, it will create a new batch. The body of the e-mail will be converted to an image and included in the batch along with any attachments. Ephesoft can even process Microsoft Office files, such as Word documents.

 You must have OpenOffice installed for this feature to process attachments other than PDF or TIF.

In order to enable processing of e-mails, edit the following file:

```
C:\Ephesoft\Application\applicationContext.xml
```

Un-comment the following lines in the configuration to appear like the following:

```
<!-- Un-comment it to start Open Office Service on this machine. -->
  <import resource="classpath:/META-INF/open-office-start-task.xml" />

<!-- Un-comment it to start Mail Module on this machine. -->
  <import resource="classpath:/META-INF/applicationContext-dcma-mail-
import.xml" />
```

In the `C:\Ephesoft\application\web-inf\classes\meta-inf\dcma-open-office\open-office.properties` file you have to change a few parameters. Change the first of the bolded parameters to be the location where OpenOffice is installed and the second to the location of the temp directory. This should be in the `Documents and Settings` folder of the OpenOffice installation user.

```
#-# Path to openoffice installation.
#-# If no path is provided, a default value will be calculated based
on the operating environment.
openoffice.homePath=C:/Program Files/OpenOffice.org 3
#-# Path to openoffice execution profile (serverType:0 only).
#-# If no path is provided, a default value will be calculated based
on the operating environment.
#-# This is always provided as absolute local path of the server
location and is always shared in case of remote conf.
openoffice.profilePath=C:/Documents and Settings/localhost/Application
Data/OpenOffice.org/3
```

Create a Windows share for the profile path on the Windows server. Also make sure that the Ephesoft user that starts the process has write access to the profile path and all subfolders.

Log in to Windows with the username that the Ephesoft process will use and launch the **OpenOffice** executable. It will prompt you to register OpenOffice. Register and then restart the Ephesoft process.

Run `netstat -a` from a command line prompt to make sure the OpenOffice process starts correctly. It should be listening on port 8100.

Once this is done, edit the batch class and go to the **Email Configuration** tab. Click on the **Add** button and enter the authentication information for the e-mail account.

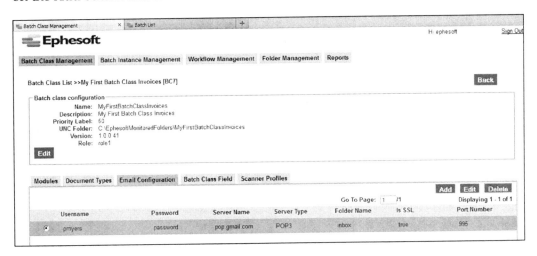

Now send an e-mail to the account specified in **Email Configuration**; Ephesoft should create a new batch instance to process the e-mail.

Summary

This concludes our investigation of document capture with Ephesoft. We started off with a review of document capture, the history of document capture, and intelligent document capture. We followed this with a tour of the Ephesoft user interface, and then walked you through the creation of a batch class and processing a batch instance. We then investigated increasingly complicated document capture problems, concluding now with some tips from experienced Ephesoft implementation professionals.

There's always more to learn, and new features being added. You should visit Ephesoft's website regularly to stay informed. We thank you for your interest, and wish you luck in your implementation.

Reference

In this appendix, we provide definitions to help you become more familiar with capture system terminology as well as tools that are specific to Ephesoft. The appendix includes the following:

- Glossary
- Common regular expressions
- Commonly modified DCMA setting

Glossary

The following terms are commonly used when implementing document capture:

- **Batch Class**: This is the definition of document types, associated fields, extraction rules, monitored folders, and e-mails for a specified workflow
- **Batch Instance**: These are the Pages being processed in the workflow
- **Classification**: This determines the type of document being processed
- **CMIS**: Content Management Interoperability Services
- **CMS**: Content Management System
- **DMS**: Document Management System, another term for CMS
- **ECM**: Enterprise Content Management, an enterprise application for managing a large volume of documents
- **Extraction**: This refers to retrieving information from documents
- **Fixed Form**: This is a type of form where the positions and dimensions of the fields are always the same

- **HA**: High Availability, a term applied to online applications, services, or technologies which are designed to be resistant to failure, and therefore always accessible

- **Hand Print**: This refers to hand-written text

- **ICR**: Intelligent Character Recognition

- **IDC**: Intelligent Document Capture

- **Indexing**: This is the process of defining field values for a particular document instance

- **KV**: A key-value pair

- **Lucene**: A full-text search engine

- **Machine Print**: This is the text that is printed by a machine (not hand-written)

- **Metadata**: This is the information about a document that is associated with that document, but not stored in the body of the document itself

- **OCR**: Optical Character Recognition

- **OOTB**: Out-of-the-box, refers to the default configuration of an application

- **Regex**: A regular expression, syntax for defining a pattern of text

- **Separation**: This is the process of determining the start and end of documents, given a set of page images

- **UI**: User Interface

- **WSDL**: Web Service Definition Language

Common regular expressions

The regular expressions used in Ephesoft are Java regular expressions. The reference documentation can be found on the Oracle website.

The following describes some more commonly used patterns:

- **Date**: [0-9]{1,2}/[0-9]{1,2}/[0-9]{2,4}

  This pattern will look for 1 or 2 digits, [0-9]{1,2}, followed by a (/) then 1 or 2 digits, [0-9]{1,2} followed by a (/) followed by 2 or 4 digits, [0-9]{2,4}. Examples of matching patterns are 1/31/12 and 03/17/1974.

- **Currency**: [0-9]{1,3}?,?[0-9]{1,3}\.[0-9]{2}

  This pattern will look for 1 to 3 digits, [0-9]{1,3}, followed by a comma (,) followed by 1 to 3 digits followed by a period (.) followed by 2 digits. The ? means 0 or 1 instance of the pattern so in this case anything followed with the ? is optional. Examples of this pattern are 20.00, 50000.00 and 600,000.00.

- **Name with Letters Only**: [a-zA-Z]{2,25}

  This pattern will look for any text that contains only upper and lower case alpha characters of 2 to 25 characters in length.

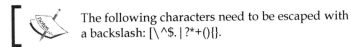

The following characters need to be escaped with a backslash: [\^$.|?*+(){}.

Commonly modified Ephesoft settings

The commonly modified settings are as follows:

dcma-workflow.properties

The number of workflow threads can be specified here. This can be changed depending on the number of cores on the Ephesoft server. If the architecture only has a single server and CPU this number may need to be lowered to have more processor availability for operators using the review and validation screens.

```
server.instance.resume.capacity=4
```

dcma-batch.properties

This file contains the configuration for batch processing.

- **batch.local_folder**: This is the location where in-process batch information and transformations are kept.
- **batch.base_http_url base url**: This is used for the location of thumbnails and preview images for the application. The host should be modified to the web host server name.

For example:

```
batch.local_folder=C:\\Ephesoft\\SharedFolders\\ephesoft-system-folder

batch.base_http_url=http://ServerA.acme.com:8080/dcma-batches
```

dcma-cmis.properties

This file has the settings for CMIS export.

- **cmis.date_format**: This is the Java date format used to transport date type fields to date attributes in CMIS. This is a global setting for all batch classes on the server. Dates must be normalized before the CMIS export.

- **cmis.document_versioning_state**: This specifies the versioning strategy for items exported from Ephesoft. Options are available as comments in the properties file.

For example:

```
cmis.date_format=MM/dd/yyyy
```

```
cmis.document_versioning_state=NONE
```

Index

FileBound export plugin 49, 85
FileNet 80
File system
  about 18, 30
  subdirectories 30
fixed form 151
Folder Management interface 25
frame busting 120
fuzzy database
  configuring 70-75

G

global CMIS configuration 82
grid computing
  about 131
  configuring 131, 132

H

HA 152
hand print 152
high speed scanners 14
history, document capture 7, 8
HOCR file 137
Hybrid Systems 11

I

IBM CM export plugin 49, 85
ICR 152
IDC 152
image classification
  about 60, 92, 93
  confidence, calculating 64
Image/Layout classification 16
import methods
  about 14
  e-mail servers 15
  Fax machines or Electronic fax servers 15
  mobile devices 16
  Print streams or EDI files 15
  scanners 14
indexing 152
intelligent document capture. See document
    capture
invoices and sales orders 13

is-mandatory tag 128
is-multivalue tag 128
is-scripting tag 128

K

Key Value Learning plugin 132
KV 152

L

LDAP 140
Lightweight Directory Access Protocol. See
    LDAP
low speed scanners 14
Lucene 152
Lucene classification 60

M

machine print 152
mapping file, DB Export 84
metadata 152
Mobile devices 16
Modules and Plugins, batch class 22
mortgage loan processing 12
Multi-Function Printer(MFP) 15

N

network attached scanners 15
no blank forms for training 137
NSI export plugin 85

O

OCR 5, 152
OOTB 152
operator user interface
  about 26
  features 26
Optical Character Recognition. See OCR
organization units. See OUs
OUs 138
overview, Active Directory 137

Thank you for buying
Intelligent Document Capture with Ephesoft

About Packt Publishing

Packt, pronounced 'packed', published its first book "*Mastering phpMyAdmin for Effective MySQL Management*" in April 2004 and subsequently continued to specialize in publishing highly focused books on specific technologies and solutions.

Our books and publications share the experiences of your fellow IT professionals in adapting and customizing today's systems, applications, and frameworks. Our solution based books give you the knowledge and power to customize the software and technologies you're using to get the job done. Packt books are more specific and less general than the IT books you have seen in the past. Our unique business model allows us to bring you more focused information, giving you more of what you need to know, and less of what you don't.

Packt is a modern, yet unique publishing company, which focuses on producing quality, cutting-edge books for communities of developers, administrators, and newbies alike. For more information, please visit our website: www.packtpub.com.

About Packt Open Source

In 2010, Packt launched two new brands, Packt Open Source and Packt Enterprise, in order to continue its focus on specialization. This book is part of the Packt Open Source brand, home to books published on software built around Open Source licences, and offering information to anybody from advanced developers to budding web designers. The Open Source brand also runs Packt's Open Source Royalty Scheme, by which Packt gives a royalty to each Open Source project about whose software a book is sold.

Writing for Packt

We welcome all inquiries from people who are interested in authoring. Book proposals should be sent to author@packtpub.com. If your book idea is still at an early stage and you would like to discuss it first before writing a formal book proposal, contact us; one of our commissioning editors will get in touch with you.

We're not just looking for published authors; if you have strong technical skills but no writing experience, our experienced editors can help you develop a writing career, or simply get some additional reward for your expertise.

LiveCode Mobile Development Beginner's Guide

ISBN: 978-1-84969-248-9   Paperback: 246 pages

Create fun-filled, rich apps for Android and iOS with LiveCode

1. Create fun, interactive apps with rich media features of LiveCode

2. Step by step instructions for creating apps and interfaces

3. Dive headfirst into mobile application development using LiveCode backed with clear explanations enriched with ample screenshots

Axure RP 6 Prototyping Essentials

ISBN: 978-1-84969-164-2   Paperback: 446 pages

Creating highly compelling, interactive prototypes with Axure that will impress and excite decision makers

1. Quickly simulate complex interactions for a wide range of applications without any programming knowledge

2. Acquire timesaving methods for constructing and annotating wireframes, interactive prototypes, and UX specifications

3. A hands-on guide that walks you through the iterative process of UX prototyping with Axure

Please check **www.PacktPub.com** for information on our titles

CPSIA information can be obtained at www.ICGtesting.com
Printed in the USA
BVOW062318030313

314587BV00003B/8/P